The Apple Does Not Fall:
A Collection of Two Plays

And Then What?
and
How Many Bushels Am I Worth?

By Bena Shklyanoy and Kevin Olson

based on Bena Shklyanoy's story of her family at https://appledoesnotfall.com/

"Touches every emotion...captivates from the moment the first lines are spoken."
-- Veronica Bruscini,
Broadway World Rhode Island review
of *And Then What?*

And Then What? Copyright 2017
How Many Bushels Am I Worth? Copyright 2018

All Rights Reserved.
Printed in the United States of America in the year 2019.
ISBN: 9781688012592

Cover Design: Tom Deja, Bossman Graphics

Special thanks: Deanna Shoss of Intercultural Talk; Amanda Siegel, Dorot Jewish Archives New York Public Library; Professor Miriam Isaacs; Ann Silverberg, Amy Olson, Katie Clements, Special Collections and Archives, Kent State University Libraries

Introduction

These plays together cover over 100 years in the lives of Bena Shklyanoy and her family. One is not a sequel to the other.

Bena's family were average folks living their lives in the times of typhus plagues, of World Wars, of Stalin's purges, of the totalitarian Soviet Union and of shortages of life's necessities – everything from milk to toilet paper.

As Jews they also suffered from pogroms and endured severe and too-often violent anti-Semitism.

This family's story serves as a master narrative of sorts for the millions and millions of Jews and others living throughout the decades of the pre-Bolshevik Russian Empire as well as the Soviet Union.

Along the way, we hope you will admire their pluck, smile and laugh at their antics and are moved by their stories and accomplishments.

These plays were originally presented by FirstHand Theatrical, a theater company I founded in 2013. FirstHand Theatrical creates original scripts based on personal, cultural and family histories.

To learn more about FirstHand Theatrical, please visit our website at firsthandtheatrical.org.

To learn more about the history of Bena's family, please visit her website at appledoesnotfall.com/

Kevin Olson
Founder and Artistic Director
FirstHand Theatrical

And Then What?
The Children of Velvel and Sheina-Gitel Averbukh©

A play
by Bena Shklyanoy and Kevin Olson

based on Bena Shklyanoy's story of her family at
https://appledoesnotfall.com/

1

DISCLAIMER REGARDING THE USE OF POEMS
INCLUDED IN THIS SCRIPT:

This script includes seven poems that are intended to be recited at various times during the play. Below are the poems we chose to use. Feel free to choose your own poems if you prefer or to not use poems at all.

However, if you want to use these poems/translations in your production, please note that, for some, you may need to obtain a license from the copyright holder. When you contact us for production rights, we will update you on the poems for which you will need to secure permission.

Due to the unknown and/or changing copyright status of the poems and/or the translations, we can provide no guarantee, warranty or indemnity with respect to the use of these poems and translations in connection with the play.

**The following poems are printed here
with permission as indicated:**

"From Here to There" by Rachel Korn, translated from the Yiddish by Seymour Mayne with Rivka Augenfeld, from *In Your Words: Translations from the Yiddish and the Hebrew* by Seymour Mayne. Ronald P. Frye & Co., 2017. Used by permission.

Molodowsky, Kadya, "At Blue Dawn, XI," *Paper Bridges: Selected Poems of Kadya Molodowsky*, translated by Kathryn Hellerstein, Wayne State University Press, 1999, p. 129. Used by permission of Kathryn Hellerstein.

Based on our research, the following poems are in the public domain.

Ivanov, Vyacheslav Ivanovich, "The Russian Mind." Translator unknown.

Rostopchina, Evdokiya, "The Unfinished Sewing." Translator unknown.

CHARACTERS

Bena – a younger woman

Khanah – Bena's great-aunt

Dinah – Bena's great-aunt

Esther – Bena's great-aunt

Polina – Bena's grandmother

Avrum – Bena's great-uncle

Kutsya – Bena's great-uncle

Leib – Bena's great-uncle

A note on casting:

The actors should be varied in their ages reflecting their stories. Leib must be taller than Avrum and Kutsya must be tall.

A note on the slides projected in the play:

Throughout the play, slides are projected. For those interested in producing the play, we can give you permission to view the slides online. Please contact us if you are interested in seeing them.

SLIDE 1 – Home page of Bena's website

A slide of the home page of Bena's website is projected as the audience enters. Slides are projected throughout the play. Their placement and content are indicated throughout the text.

Upstage on either side of the screen are two coat trees. An empty and open old suitcase sits on the floor downstage. Center-stage is a small desk table with a chair. Seven matching chairs for the siblings are placed around the stage as desired.

The siblings should be costumed reflecting their personalities and the different time periods in which their stories are set, ranging from the late 1800s through the early 1970s. On the coat trees are accessories which the siblings will put on as each is introduced for their story.

Those accessories can include hats, caps, ties, scarves, aprons, jewelry etc. An old Russian book in an avoska (string bag) should be placed on a coat tree to be used in Leib's story as well as a white pinafore and a red neck scarf that Bena will put on towards the end of the play. Bena should be costumed in attractive but plain and somewhat old-fashioned, drab and darkish clothing.

Quiet music based on Russian, Yiddish and Soviet melodies is played as the poems are recited and at other times as appropriate and effective.

SCENE 1

BENA: For some, the apple does not fall far from the tree. But my grandmother said that because you belong to a family the apple really does not fall at all. You don't ever need to see them; you don't even need to know them; you are always part of that family.

SLIDE 2 – Rakhil, Bena's mother

My name is Bena. The day my mother died in 2004, it stunned me that my older daughter did not recognize the keepsakes and the cracked murky photos buried in her grandmother's closets. "How would I know?" she asked. She was amazed that I had expected genetics on its own to transport memories.

Emily's simple question jarred me into the realization that many invaluable threads of our security blanket and chunks of our armor — our family history — would be lost on my watch unless I fortified them through stories, pictures, documents, historical markers.

SLIDE 3 -- Family tree

I am an only child as was my mother. With my mother's death, I was now at the top of my branch of the family tree. I set out to save the slivers of my family story not blotted out by the merciless 20th century and alas by my own lack of curiosity.

I started researching family roots, meeting many new cousins, writing down my family story, and collecting photographs. The more I learned the more it felt as if I was conjuring their presence and as if they were speaking directly to me.

SLIDE 4 – Velvel and Sheina-Gitel, Bena's great-grandparents

So, permit me to "conjure" for you one branch of my tree — the children of my great-grandparents Velvel Averbukh and Sheina-Gitel Kupperschmidt.

In 1879, Velvel and Sheina-Gitel saw each other for the first time at their chuppah - wedding canopy. Their fathers had arranged the marriage only a short time before. Sheina-Gitel gave birth 17 times over a 25-year period. But only seven children reached adulthood — nine died as infants or toddlers and one daughter at the age of 16.

SLIDE 5 – The 7 Children of Velvel and Sheina-Gitel

Those who made it past 16 years are my three great-aunts — Khanah, Dinah and Esther; my three great-uncles — Avrum, Yankel-Shmul and Leib; and my dear grandmother Polina.

Sadly, I do not have a photo of my Great-Uncle Yankel-Shmul who was called Kutsya. So, I am using a photo of my Great-Uncle Leib as a young man who I'm told Kutsya sort of looked like at that age. Researching family is not an exact science as I learned.

SLIDE 6 – Belaya Tserkov

KHANAH: Our Tateh and Mameh — Velvel and Sheina-Gitel — grew up in nearby towns inside the Pale of Settlement – the Jewish ghetto established by Catherine the Great. These towns were called *shtetls*. With few exceptions, Jews were not allowed to live in the big cities of the Russian Empire. Tateh and Mameh lived their married life in Tateh's hometown of Belaya Tserkov, where we were all born.

SLIDE 7 – Sheina-Gitel, Bena's great-grandmother

DINAH: Mameh made certain that each of her children memorized the Hebrew alphabet by 2 years old and read Yiddish fluently by 4. Her daughters remained in her charge while her sons graduated into Tateh's home schooling.

ESTHER: For a woman reared in a poor *shtetl* family, Mameh possessed an uncanny sense of etiquette and dignity. She coached the children on the proper way to enter and exit a room, how to address people of different ages and status, how to unobtrusively change a topic, and how to say yes or no with eyes and body language.

SLIDE 8 – Market in Belaya Tserkov and a *tichel*

POLINA: When more income was needed, Mameh sold *tichels* -- head coverings for Jewish women -- from clothing stalls at the market in Belaya Tserkov. She was an entrepreneur and her business became a reliable source of income.

SLIDE 9 – Velvel, Bena's great-grandfather

AVRUM: It was said of Tateh -- never proven -- that he was descended from a prominent Rabbinic dynasty dating back to 15th century Germany – The Averbukh Rabbinic Dynasty. This etching resembles how he looked and dressed -- this man is almost a spitting image of him.

KUTSYA: Tateh was a *melamed* – a teacher. He taught at the yeshiva and took in private pupils, boys who strove to expand their Torah knowledge. His presence and legacy loomed large in the lives of his children and their descendants.

LEIB: Tateh's philosophy and household principles were more like commandments passed through enough generations to enter the genome of all his descendants. His remarkable intuition bordered on clairvoyance. He always challenged his children to look beyond the immediate. His catch phrase was:

ENSEMBLE: *(in unison)* "Suppose you prevail – *Und Vus Veiter*. And then what?"

BENA: Growing up hearing my grandmother's constant refrain — "as my Tateh used to say" — I myself cannot keep a conversation going without interjecting at some point:

"As my great-grandfather used to say -- Suppose you prevail. And then what?"

(The Ensemble sits save Khanah.)

SCENE 2

SLIDE 10 – Khanah

(As Bena introduces her, Khanah moves to one of the two coat trees and puts on her costume accessories.)

BENA: My great-aunt Khanah was the first-born. She got her business smarts from Sheina-Gitel and her wavy hair, large eyes, and sense of superiority from Velvel.

Khanah cut her Queen Bee teeth bossing her siblings around. Being the oldest girl offered tangible advantages – she got to wear clothes though used but before they got passed down to her sisters.

SLIDE 11 – Lapti and 19th century "real shoes"

It was for her that the first pair of real shoes, not the usual *lapti*, the straw shoes the family wore most of the time, was acquired in anticipation of a *shidduch*. At the first whisper that she became available on the marriage market, offers began coming in.

KHANAH: Tateh turned down anybody who asked for a dowry. For the candidates he deemed worthy of meeting in person, Tateh conducted the appropriate *derfragen* — background check based on the town's grapevine — that included against his better judgment the financial standing of the prospective husband — something I insisted he do.

BENA: The few that progressed to the finals visited with the family.

KHANAH: Tateh made his preference known but asked for my consent. The young man who swept me off my feet was not Tateh's first choice.
  (sighing)
But oh, he carried a walking stick under his arm and wore a modern top hat.

Tateh said yes and with the marriage agreement signed, I and my intended went *spazieren* -- for a walk -- unchaperoned, in full view of Belaya Tserkov. I wore my real shoes for the first time.

SLIDE 12 – Samovar

But I returned from that walk in tears. Tateh, I said, he is cheap! He is a fool! He wants me to use firewood to heat the samovar only if we <u>both</u> want tea. What if only I want tea?

I knew then and there that this marriage would be a mistake. So Tateh immediately put in motion the annulment procedure to break our agreement. Suddenly, my *yikhes* — lineage —, my good looks, and my superior brain no longer counted for much. I was now damaged goods.

Tateh predicted that I would eventually marry but would not have children.

SLIDE 13 – Khanah

BENA: Every year that passed, more and more questions about Khanah's character, mental stability and other attributes made arranging a marriage that much more painful, if not hopeless. And Velvel did not offer up his daughters – they were to be sought after!

Khanah was 24 when Velvel received a visitor from the nearby town of Boguslav. Khaim Melamed, an eager scholar and a mediocre fish wholesaler, had lost his wife in childbirth and was looking for a bride. Following a discussion of Khaim's requirements, Velvel invited him to join the Sabbath meal.

KHANAH: The next day Khaim asked Tateh for my hand and I consented.

SLIDE 14 – Market in Belaya Tserkov

BENA: Before leaving to settle in Boguslav with her husband, Khanah made sure that people saw her purchasing new clothes and shoes at the market:

KHANAH: "Eat Your Heart Out" Belaya Tserkov!

BENA: Khanah took nothing from her parents' home. And she left that first pair of real shoes for my Grandmother — her sister Polina — the next-bride-to-be in a family where all the girls had bigger feet than Khanah.

SLIDE 15 – Boguslav

KHANAH: In Boguslav, I took over managing the business and restricted Khaim's activity to what he did expertly: selling fish. The business thrived.

BENA: Prosperous and in a position of power, Khanah mellowed to such a degree that she promised her sisters swanky bedcovers if they married into money. If not, no gift would make a difference anyway. A dozen years later, in the face of the Bolshevik Revolution, she made Khaim sell the business.

KHANAH: I converted the proceeds into gold coins that I sewed into hidden pockets on my clothing and into small items of silverware kept in a wicker basket mixed in with what looked like rags.

SLIDE 16 – Soviet flag

BENA: They were now living in the Soviet Union, not the Tsarist ruled Russian Empire.

KHANAH: Gold coins and other valuables would be confiscated and we would be arrested for keeping funds from the government. Owning private property was abolished, but single-family houses could remain in private hands, so we were allowed to stay in our house in Boguslav.

SLIDE 17 – House in Boguslav

BENA: But…during the Great Patriotic War as the Soviets called World War II, Khanah and Khaim evacuated to Siberia to escape the Nazi invaders. Jews who remained in Boguslav were murdered by the Nazis or by their neighbors. Khanah and Khaim's house was taken over.

KHANAH: After the war, we had nothing to go back to.

SLIDE 18 – Kiev 1947

BENA: Khanah's sister Polina, my grandmother, arranged a residency permit for them in Kiev.

KHANAH: My stash of gold coins helped us buy a large dilapidated room in a two-room communal apartment on the far outskirts of Kiev. Don't ask me who I bribed or how much. We were lucky – we only had to live with one other family.

SLIDE 19 – A typical communal apartment

BENA: Most of these communal apartments had from five to over a dozen rooms. And rarely did a family have more than one of those rooms to themselves. The kitchen and the bath facilities, if indoor, were shared with everyone. Khaim worked as a clerk at a factory for wages barely sufficient to pay for cigarettes.

KHANAH: If not for the injections from my stash, we would have had to depend on handouts from my siblings, a position I could not accept.

SLIDE 20 –Bena's actual baby gifts from Khanah

BENA: Khanah marked my entrance into the world with gifts to me of a silver teaspoon, a baby silver fork, and a thumb-size silver shot glass. Each of them is alive and well and in need of polishing.

KHANAH: I was in Odessa visiting my sister Esther the summer you were born. I told your mother to send me a telegram if the baby was a boy but a letter if it was a girl.

BENA: Always the Queen Bee, Khanah was loyal and dedicated to our family. My warmest childhood memories are of Khanah arriving on weekends with a chunk of halvah from the market and a fresh baguette. We ate with such gusto and such love for each other that sixty years later and long after her passing, I can still taste that mouthwatering halvah and feel the love radiating from her large black eyes behind funny thin-rimmed round glasses.

SLIDE 21 – Khanah's grave site

Khanah died when I was 8 years old. No silverware remained but there were enough gold coins in her secret pockets to erect a granite tombstone. Khanah and Khaim were married for over 40 years. But as Velvel predicted, they were childless.

SLIDE 22 – Khanah

KHANAH: *(Walking slowly towards the suitcase placed downstage, she recites "At Blue Dawn, XI" by Kadya Molodowsly, translated by Kathryn Hellerstein. See page 2. Her photo stays up throughout the poem. Music underscores the poem.)*

I have come out of darkness and hiding,
And my small feet
Take large strides.
And my thin fists
Knock loud and strong.

I have come out of darkness and hiding.
I wash my hands,
Raising my eyes to the sun for the first time,
And light the candles for the festival of the world,
Candles that were piously lit
For generations.

I take steps of light
And, with festive colors, dye
The threads that I'm weaving in and out.

(When she finishes, she places the costume accessories she removed from the coat tree into the suitcase.)

SCENE 3

SLIDE 23 – Avrum

(As Bena introduces him, Avrum moves to one of the two coat trees and puts on his costume accessories.)

BENA: I never met my Great-Uncle Avrum, Velvel and Sheina-Gitel's oldest son. He was Velvel's equal in ability and was home schooled by him – Velvel's pride and hope.

AVRUM: Tateh's pupils disappointed him. He warned me never to become a teacher. No profession is less rewarding he said: "you give your heart to convey precious knowledge, but it doesn't penetrate your pupils' minds. All you get at the end of the day are a sore throat and not enough money to put food on the table."

But then he added, "Remember that every Averbukh branch produced at least one *melamed*."

I was the heir apparent to the "Averbukh Rabbinic Dynasty." But my teenage years fell at the chaotic start of the 20th century in the Russian Empire. For me and most Jewish youth cooped up in *shtetls*, the urge to annihilate the old order took priority over everything else.

SLIDE 24 – Anarchy poster

BENA: Of the many ideologies vying for an audience, Avrum was drawn to anarchism.

AVRUM: I participated in clandestine gatherings, wrote fiery leaflets in Yiddish against the Tsar and the Empire, and improved my Russian to translate anarchist literature into Yiddish. Tateh did not know of my involvement in these endeavors but he incessantly disapproved of nonsense that called for utter destruction before attempting to envision a —oh, I can still hear him:

"Suppose you prevail. And then what?"

Socialist, Bolshevik, anarchist—labels meant nothing to him. Passionate revolutionary speeches made no sense to him. As far as he was concerned, such talk could lead to nothing good, considering that the fervent people listening to those speeches were the uneducated and the gullible. "They'll throw aside tradition – and then what?"

One night, the Russian gendarmes trashed our house looking for me.
    (slyly)
Conveniently I was not home. They turned over the featherbed searching for my leaflets, rummaged in the oven, and—the ultimate insult! — rifled through Tateh's books.

SLIDE 25 –Soviet religion propaganda poster

But I was not swayed by Tateh's fury over the desecrated books. I lectured him on the merits of anarchism and recommended he walk away from the doomed world of yesterday, along with its Torah, and start reading more relevant literature.

He berated me: "Now you are an anarchist, then you'll become a

17

socialist, then you'll become a murderer." At that time, I did not realize that this insight into his country's future was far too visionary for most of us, drunk on utopian dreams, to comprehend.

SLIDE 26 – Avrum and Rose

BENA: Velvel was also displeased that Avrum had found a bride on his own, a daughter of a *balmalukhe* – a menial worker.

AVRUM: He believed this marriage diminished my chance of having scholarly offspring further threatening the Averbukh Dynasty. He said, "He who descends from a cat is doomed to meow." And he could not forgive that I turned my back on tradition. You see, I was not just a son but a shining star, an heir to everything Tateh held sacred.

I could no longer take his constant badgering. So in 1906, I followed my bride Rose's family to the United States and ended up in Philadelphia. I changed my name to Abraham Auerbach and raised three children.

SLIDE 27 – *Der Tog*, Yiddish Newspaper

I worked third shift at a factory as a weaver and a presser. During the day, I wrote. The New York Yiddish newspaper *Der Tog*, The Day, published my short stories. My wife constantly nagged

BENA: *(arms akimbo; Jewish intonation)* "We have nothing to eat and you write!"

AVRUM: My sister Polina wrote me that Tateh pretended not to hear when Mameh read my letters home out loud. Once, reacting to my admission that perhaps I had been overly enamored with anarchism, he commented:

SLIDE 28 – Avrum and Rose

BENA: *(heavenward)* "Why did I have to lose my son and he to travel so far to understand such a simple thing? "

AVRUM: In later years, I became an insurance agent and taught at Gratz College, a school for Jewish studies in Philadelphia—a teacher, after all. Anarchism discarded, I turned to Zionism and spent several months in Israel in the early 1960s.

There, I had expected a show of reverence that befitted the heir of the renowned Averbukh Rabbinical Dynasty. But my lineage elicited barely any recognition.

SLIDE 29 – Letter from an unknown cousin

BENA: Shortly before his death, Avrum completed the Averbukh family history, a fact uncovered a half-century later in a letter sent by an unknown cousin to one of Avrum's children.

That cousin intended to publish Avrum's manuscript which had been left with him for safekeeping, but he died before he could do it. The manuscript was lost.

SLIDE 30 – Avrum's grave site

Avrum died in Philadelphia in 1963. When Avrum came to Philadelphia in 1906, he emigrated from the Pale of Settlement, the home of the Jews portrayed in "Fiddler on the Roof."

SLIDE 31 – Rakhil, Polina's daughter, with Ruth, Avrum's daughter

In 1975, twelve years after Avrum's death, the first of the old-country Averbukhs immigrated to the United States and sought out their Auerbach cousins.

For at least 40 years, Soviet authorities had blocked correspondence between these family branches. The Iron Curtain had descended.

So, the children and grandchildren of Pale of Settlement immigrants who were born in the United States mistakenly imagined their Soviet cousins who arrived in the U.S. beginning in the 1970s – like me -- to be *frum* -- religious folk -- from olden-days stories and old-country pictures.

SLIDE 32 – Reunion of cousins

But when our American cousins finally met us, they met a Jew not at all like the image they held. We wore modern clothes, we were educated, we were secular and we were completely ignorant of Jewish

AVRUM: *(sings like Tevye in "Fiddler on the Roof")* "Tradition."

SLIDE 33 – Avrum

AVRUM: *(Walking slowly towards the suitcase placed downstage, he recites "Ships That Sail Forth" by Yury Terapiano, translated by Bradley Jordan. See page 2. His photo stays up throughout the poem. Music underscores the poem.)*

Ships that sail forth,
Trains that speed away,
Remaining in the distance,
Forever forsaken!

The shores can no longer be seen;
As you turn from them, I dare you,
To love (if you can) your enemies,
To forget (if you can) your friends.

(When he finishes, he places the costume accessories he removed from the coat tree into the suitcase.)

SCENE 4

SLIDE 34 – Dinah

(As Bena introduces her, Dinah moves to one of the two coat trees and puts on her costume accessories.)

BENA: My Great-Aunt Dinah shared her large eyes with her father and her serene disposition with her mother. But nobody could tie her exotic gypsy or Indian looks to any known lineage – except possibly the world-wide Averbukh Rabbinic Dynasty.

Dinah did not actively crave learning but became the first Averbukh child and the first girl to receive formal education in an era that forbade educating girls.

DINAH: Tateh would always say:

BENA: "What does she need an education for?"

SLIDE 35 – Dinah and Khanah

DINAH: But my sister, Khanah — the Queen-Bee — 19 years older than me and married, thought differently. She hatched a scheme to enroll me into a Jewish elementary school for girls and then into *gymnasia* — high school — for girls in Boguslav where she lived. The deal made with Tateh was that after high school I would return home to Belaya Tserkov to get married.

BENA: Dinah's graduation from high school coincided with the peak of revolutionary destruction, pogroms and the typhus epidemics.

DINAH: Khanah refused to let me out of her sight, much less travel; even showing up in the street was dangerous. Consequently, I did not return to my parents' home to find a husband as originally agreed.

But being vigilant did not mean keeping me from the company of lovesick males — meaning Khanah now had an opportunity to shine as a matchmaker.

SLIDE 36 – Yankel Smetanin, Dinah's first husband

Shine she did! A match was made -- Yankel Smetanin, a merchant's son, was older than me, dashing and fancy mustached. He was in line to get half of his parents' house as my letter to Tateh reported.

I also wrote that Khanah promised to give me silver candlesticks and a swanky bedcover, further testimony that my beloved came from money. But by the time my letter to Tateh asking permission to marry was delivered by the unreliable mail service, I was already married.

BENA: Dinah lost her husband to typhus when their baby daughter, Khaya, was only 6 weeks old. She had to move back in with her sister Khanah and spent the next three years supported by Khanah's gold coins.

SLIDE 37 – Leningrad

DINAH: Because of the recent pogroms, Khanah decided that I should get out of the *shtetl* and that the best way to do that was by finding a husband who lived in a big city. She asked a cousin in Leningrad for help and as soon as a candidate emerged there, we took a week-long train journey to deliver me and my Khaya to meet him.

SLIDE 38 – Dinah, Khaya and Levenstein

He worked as an office clerk, an ordinary-looking man, balding, shorter than me and much older. His last name was Levenstein.

He had settled in Leningrad several years before, after a pogrom in his *shtetl* had wiped out his family. Terrible -- while his wife and children were being murdered, he was out of the house checking up on his parents; as he was running back home through a wooded path, his parents were murdered.
    (long pause)
Khanah set out to learn all about Levenstein. She approved, for the most part, but was skeptical about his love for chess and his stomach ulcers. It did not take long for Levenstein to propose perhaps out of empathy for me as much as attraction. We shared much sadness.

BENA: In doing my research, we could find no record of Levenstein's first name. So Levenstein he is...

DINAH: Since religious ceremonies were now prohibited in the Soviet Union, we registered our marriage at a government office and then took a streetcar to Levenstein's small room in a communal apartment in the far outskirts of Leningrad.

In this new life, I spent my days in search of food to ensure that Levenstein got fresh meals right out of the oven and that Khaya was well nourished.

SLIDE 39 – Siege of Leningrad

When the Eastern front of World War II reached us on June 22 of 1941, my daughter was 19 years old. Khaya had grown into a brave adult -- she had to be.

By September, the German army encircled Leningrad. It was stopped a short distance from our apartment building. Bombs and bullets fell close by every day. As the siege continued, food rations shrank to next to nothing. Despite my valiant efforts, Levenstein soon died of hunger.

SLIDE 40 – Lake Ladoga evacuation

That winter the Red Army carved out a route over frozen Lake Ladoga to bring supplies and munitions into Leningrad and to evacuate civilians out of the city. In the spring of 1942, I joined the crowd gathered by the dock hoping to eventually get on a boat with my daughter and escape the Siege of Leningrad.

SLIDE 41 – Bomb crater on Leningrad street

While I waited on the line to board a boat to safety, Khaya's job was to get our daily bread ration. This was hunger time. No one had energy and even walking was a chore. But so many thousands and thousands of us did what we had to do to survive.

BENA: One day when Khaya arrived with the bread ration for her mother, she was told that Dinah had died of hunger the night before and had already been taken away for burial in a mass grave. My Great-Aunt Dinah died three years before I was born.

SLIDE 42 – Dinah

DINAH: *(Walking slowly towards the suitcase placed downstage, she recites "From Here To There" by Rachel Korn, translated by Seymour Mayne with Rifka Augenfeld. See page 2. Her photo stays up throughout the poem. Music underscores the poem.)*

From here
to there –
is it far?
just a step.

Everything is prepared,
all is ready:
even the angel
with wings folded
like tired arms,
waits at the crossroads of time
to kiss my forehead
that I should forget all,
that I should become
like him,
without smile,
sadness,
or tears.

(When she finishes, she places the costume accessories she removed from the coat tree into the suitcase.)

SCENE 5

SLIDE 43 – Kutsya

(As Bena introduces him, Kutsya moves to one of the two coat trees and puts on his costume accessories.)

BENA: His siblings unanimously loved my Great-Uncle Yankel-Shmul, Kutsya, the most. They described him as:

KHANAH: the handsomest,

DINAH: the tallest,

ESTHER: the brightest,

POLINA: the wittiest,

BENA: and the gentlest. The mention of his name lit up his sisters' faces. Normally undemonstrative, they reminisced about him with wide smiles, teenage excitement and an envy reserved for the naughty.

SLIDE 44 – Cheder students

KUTSYA: And naughty I was—pranks, jokes, somersaults — anything to avoid studying. Forced by Tateh to spend hours over books, I fidgeted and jumped up and down and wrote lyrics that made fun of my sisters. Spanking did not help. Mameh defended me to Tateh:

BENA: "What's the use of staring at a book?"

KUTSYA: But Tateh always got the last word:

BENA: "One must look inside a prayer book. His brain will retain something."

SLIDE 45 – 19th century fabric

KUTSYA: Unlike my brother Avrum, I had no interest in revolution or politics. I inherited my paternal grandfather's gift for evaluating fabric by touch. I started making money after my bar mitzvah.

Being a responsible businessman, however, did not prevent me from churning out verses mocking my customers who did not always appreciate my sense of humor and complained to Tateh. But even the complainers could not resist my charm.

Also unlike Avrum, I let Tateh find a match for me. Khaya was a rabbi's orphan from another *shtetl* and was as timid as I was mischievous. She fell in love with me at first sight.

BENA: "And who would not fall in love with him," his sisters asked rhetorically.

SLIDE 46 – Illustration of a wedding procession

KUTSYA: We had a proper and traditional wedding. In less than two years Khaya gave birth to our two boys who, Mameh was relieved to observe, showed no propensity for naughtiness.

BENA: Tragically, they both died quite young of typhus.

KUTSYA: But then, conscription time for the Tsar's Army came -- a 20 year enlistment. Long-term guests of the Russian Empire, we *shtetl* Jews had developed a laundry list of methods to avoid being drafted, some of them more extreme than others.

Most of these methods involved going into permanent hiding or pretending to be an invalid to convince the medical committee that you were physically not able to serve. Whether you were drafted and even where you were assigned was based on how healthy you looked.

SLIDE 47 – Tsar's Imperial Guard

And, my good looks, God save me, likely would have qualified me for the Imperial Guard. Twenty-year enlistment? No way. After much consideration of various methods to avoid the draft, I chose the easiest and, rumor had it, sure-fire recipe. It was definitely less dramatic than amputating a toe which some people did.

I drank some vinegar to cause my skin to yellow thereby getting certified as ineligible. After which I just needed to wait for skin to clear. Little did I know that an Averbukh should not take for granted his liver.

BENA: So, while Kutsya did manage to dodge the draft, his skin did not clear. He died a few months later at the age of 27. Vinegar never entered an Averbukh home in the old country again.

SLIDE 48 – Kutsya

KUTSYA: *(Walking slowly towards the suitcase placed downstage, he recites "The Banks of a River" by Abraham Sutzkever, translated by Ruth Whitman. See page 2. His photo stays up throughout the poem. Music underscores the poem.)*

From a high mountain,
I see how the banks of a river shimmer.

I look down
into the river where my face's tinder is quenched and my body
shines clear, transparent, and I say to the east, west, north, south:

Look and see
How beneath choked leaves and houses
In cold riverwriting my name is written.

Broadcast it all over the world.

Amen.

(When he finishes, he places the costume accessories he removed from the coat tree into the suitcase.)

SCENE 6

SLIDE 49 – Esther

(As Bena introduces her, Esther moves to one of the two coat trees and puts on her costume accessories.)

BENA: I knew my Great-Aunt Esther well. She visited us in Kiev almost every year. We were quite fond of each other. Esther was the baby, born after a five-year gap caused by an infection. Esther joked that thankfully:

ESTHER: *(still at the coat tree)* Mameh got cured — and I was born!

BENA: She had a legendary sense of humor and laughed contagiously. Had she been the oldest, Esther would have made a consummate Queen Bee. Being the youngest she had no choice but to take the opposite path.

ESTHER: I loved how my siblings pampered me and how young men admired me. I was the most attractive of the Averbukh girls. Few chores were expected of me, so I spent most of my time reading and giggling with my girlfriends.

I graduated from *gymnasia* for girls with a gold medal. But I did not contemplate further studies or seek an office job given my academic accomplishments. After all, a husband of a gorgeous and genius girl would be so honored to have me that he would not let me work.

SLIDE 50 – Esther and Srul

And as it turned out, in my late teens, I married Srul, an

intelligent hardworking man. Oh, how I mocked his appearance; he was stooped, not very tall, wearing thick glasses—yet nobody would have loved me more.

BENA: After receiving his graduate degree, Srul was placed as chief engineer at a factory in a small Ukrainian town; it was the number two position.

SLIDE 51 – Esther, Valya and Srul

ESTHER: The factory assigned him a chauffeured car and half of a house requisitioned from a laborer. The laborer's wife babysat our little girl, Valya, named after Tateh who had died six years earlier in 1922.

My husband, warm, kindhearted and unassuming, was well-liked. I took every advantage of his reputation and my second-lady status. I entertained the factory and the town bigwigs; had Srul's chauffeur take me shopping to the larger town; had the laborers' wives cook and clean for me.

BENA: But their privileged life ended abruptly in the beginning of 1930s. Srul's superiors had the decency to warn him that he was going to be arrested for spying on behalf of Japan and that Esther and Valya were going to be sent into exile. Supposedly spies were everywhere during these times; it did not matter what country you were "spying" for since it was all Stalin's invention.

SLIDE 52 – Odessa

ESTHER: The night Srul was warned, our landlord took us to the train station. We boarded a train to Odessa where Srul had friends. We were safe for the time being. The authorities did not pursue those who were not home at arrest time since it was not like the charges were real.

SLIDE 53 – Odessa steps

In Odessa, Srul found a teaching job at a technical college. The job paid little and had no perks for me. But Odessa, being a cultural city with a significant Jewish population, gave me the opportunity to gather a few Jewish writers and scientists -- my intellectual salon.

We met regularly to discuss art, literature, philosophy and so on. But Stalin's purges promptly snuffed out the life of my salon as well as the life of most of its participants. Thankfully, their association with Srul and me never came to light.

SLIDE 54 – Esther and Srul with their children, Valya and Gregory

BENA: During this anxious period, their son Gregory was born. The ritual circumcision, *bris*, was not yet officially banned in the Soviet Union. But it was becoming much less common because of fear of punishment, or fear of marking the son as religious, or a lack of *mohels* to perform it, or the increasingly progressive views of parents.

ESTHER: I came up with a plot to give Gregory a bris that would protect Srul's job -- we hoped.

He went away on a business trip. I placed the baby in a wicker basket and took a train to a *shtetl* where an old *mohel* still functioned, albeit by trusted references only; Srul would return home "shocked" to discover what his insubordinate wife had done in his absence and without his knowledge.

That was the scenario that we were going to stick with if found out. Whether it would have saved us had we been reported was anybody's guess.

SLIDE 55 – Train evacuation

BENA: When World War II began, Srul's poor eyesight kept him from being drafted. The technical college where he taught evacuated its staff who were not draft eligible to Siberia, including Srul along with Esther, Gregory and Valya, who was not well.

ESTHER: Srul was drafted eventually. But since he could only see a couple of meters in front of him, he could not be trusted with a weapon. They used his math skills to calculate canon projectiles.
> *(sad chuckle)*

But they had to lead him by hand from one position to the next so he would not wander off. The Army discharged him after three months.

SLIDE 56 – Valya

Meanwhile, I concentrated on caring for my children, especially Valya who was showing symptoms of kidney disease. She was getting worse and I did all I knew to do and could do....
> *(Pause)*

She was 15 when she died.

BENA: After the war Esther, Srul and Gregory returned to Odessa. She never completely recovered from the loss of her daughter and became surly, sullen, susceptible to brief frenetic

34

bursts of energy and fierce man-chasing that panicked her siblings.

SLIDE 57 – Polina and Esther

When Esther came to visit us in Kiev, each visit began with her bawling on Polina's shoulders. By the time they finished talking, Esther was pouting and it was Polina who was crying. Polina could not forgive her baby-sister for wasting the brilliant academic abilities that nature gave her.

SLIDE 58 -- Srul and Esther

In 1975, Esther and Srul, both in poor health, arrived in San Francisco. Gregory had immigrated there earlier that year. They were the third family of Soviet Jews to be re-settled in San Francisco as part of the "Save Soviet Jewry" movement.

SLIDE 59 – Esther

ESTHER: *(Walking slowly towards the suitcase placed downstage, she recites "Reverie" by Rayzel Zuchlinska, translated by Marc Kaminsky. See page 2. Her photo stays up throughout the poem. Music underscores the poem.)*

The clothes in which you saw me –
they'll never get old,
with all their colors
they go on blossoming in my closet.

The violet dress is whispering to the green
a green and grassy secret.

35

And Then What?

The rose clings to the yellow
and at their hems
flowers continue to blossom.

Removed and special in a corner of its own,
its arms thrown over its shoulders,
my blue dress is dreaming of you.

(When she finishes, she places the costume accessories she removed from the coat tree into the suitcase.)

SCENE 7

SLIDE 60 – Leib

(As Bena introduces him Leib moves to one of the two coat trees and puts on his costume accessories.)

BENA: I knew my Great-Uncle Leib very well having spent considerable time with him for much of my life in the Soviet Union.

Taller than his oldest brother Avrum, Leib was like him in appearance and intellect. Gratified to have a scholarly son again, Velvel was, however, deprived of the chance to homeschool him. It was a different world – a world of Revolution. Jewish education was unwanted and useless. Young Jews like Leib craved a secular education.

Leib chose to attend *gymnasia*, secular high school, not Velvel's "academy."

And he did not ask permission to do so! He graduated with a gold medal, straight "A"s, and was especially fond of literature. He read all the time.

SLIDE 61 -- Leningrad

LEIB: Letters from a cousin in the far-away city of Leningrad made me yearn for the library book shelves and university lectures there. But Tateh would be crushed if he lost me.

After Tateh's funeral, Mameh told me to go to Leningrad already. Jews could live in big cities following the Revolution.

SLIDE 62 – Soviet Proletarian poster

BENA: Leib enrolled in an engineering college. "Everyone" had the right to an education now but only if they belonged to the Proletariat. The rest, like Leib, had to take tests and hope for vacant spots. He got in but he wondered what would happen when the laborers and peasants graduated and were no longer considered Proletarians.

LEIB: I so wanted to say to them: "So you've prevailed. Now what?" But it was not a time that encouraged questions or, God forbid, doubts.

BENA: He sensed that asking his questions would be considered dangerous if not incendiary. Leib dropped out of college and vowed to stay away from the new order.

SLIDE 63 – Nevsky Prospect

LEIB: I found clerical work; rented a bed in someone's room; walked several kilometers once a month to a post office to ship food to Mameh; strolled down Nevsky Prospect taking in the architecture; and I read, hungrily, eagerly.

I was quickly promoted to a bookkeeping position and married a golden-haired librarian, a deacon's daughter.

BENA: Leib did not share his marital news with his family nor the news about the birth of his son. Sheina-Gitel could handle anything except the knowledge that her son married outside the faith and that her grandson was not Jewish. But their son died quite young and he and his wife divorced a year later.

SLIDE 64 – Entrance to a communal apartment

Leib rented an inexpensive room in a 9-room communal apartment. Six different families occupied six of the rooms. Another family of previously high aristocratic status occupied the other rooms and rented one out to make ends meet.

Before the Revolution all nine rooms belonged to them. But after the Revolution, their status became *lishentsy* – people who were deprived of their rights and property.

SLIDE 65 – Musya and Leib

LEIB: The oldest child in this family was Maria, nicknamed Musya. As I got to know her, we realized we liked each other a great deal. During our secret courtship, she admitted to me that her "distinguished formerly aristocratic" family held their collective nose where Jews were concerned.

A personal relationship with a Jew was unthinkable; particularly with a renter; and particularly with a renter born of uneducated parents from a backwater town.

But -- we decided to marry. Musya chose her birthday party to make the announcement to her family. I attended as well.

Her family and friends had all met me and liked me but in the abstract way people liked a servant. And they were taken aback by my presence at their table. When she announced that we were engaged, the refined company did not react visibly.

Musya's mother covered her face with her fan. But her youngest sister, Katya, nodded approvingly.

One of the cousins said mockingly:

"I have to tell you, Leib, your manners are impeccable.
May I ask who taught you manners?"

I responded courteously: "My illiterate mother." Musya's relatives
never mocked me again.

BENA: Sheina-Gitel did not learn about Leib's second marriage
either though his sisters knew. To them, Musya remained a
respected but alien wife of a beloved brother.

SLIDE 66 – Leib, 1945

After the war, Leib worked as head bookkeeper at an engineering
firm. Soon after his retirement Musya began exhibiting symptoms
of dementia.

LEIB: I took care of her until she required lifting. She did not
recognize me any longer but I visited her at the nursing home
every day, in any weather, for three years, until her last day.

SLIDE 67 – Train station in Leningrad

BENA: My first time in Leningrad was in January 1962 during my
high school winter break. My visit coincided with the first day of
Leib's retirement. These were the years of Khrushchev's "Thaw"
when the political and cultural climate in the Soviet Union
relaxed.

Yevtushenko's galvanizing poem *Babi Yar* had just been published
– a miracle. Like so many others, especially those my age, I knew

the poem by heart. As I waited in the train station for Leib to meet me, I recited *Babi Yar* to myself again and again.

SLIDE 68 – Partial text of *Babi Yar*

It ended with these stirring words:

(Recites stirringly in Russian only if the actor is fluent in Russian.)

Интернационал
        пусть прогремит,
когда навеки похоронен будет
последний на земле антисемит.
Еврейской крови нет в крови моей.
Но ненавистен злобой заскорузлой

    всем антисемитам,
        как еврей,
и   потому —
я   настоящий русский!

Yevtushenko's poem rang out like a bell summoning people's consciousness – the word Jew uttered in public, uttered with respect, uttered with compassion, printed for everyone to see.

When Leib arrived, I recited the poem for him. He watched and listened with a patronizing smile:

(Recites stirringly in English.)

"May 'Internationale' thunder and ring
When, for all time, is buried and forgotten
The last of anti-Semites on this earth.

41

There is no Jewish blood that's blood of mine,
But, hated with a passion that's corrosive
Am I by anti-Semites like a Jew.
And that is why I call myself a Russian!"

In my exhilaration, I proclaimed that we had entered a
Renaissance, not merely Khrushchev's "Thaw." Leib raised his
brows above his glasses.

LEIB: Sure. After 40-year entombment, a mat to sleep on is the
Renaissance. Poems will come and arrests will be fewer. And then
what? We still wait for the Party to tell us how to think.

SLIDE 69 – Yevtushenko recites *Babi Yar*

BENA: It took my tears to get him to take me to a reading by
Yevtushenko. But – another miracle -- he liked what he heard and
got swept up in the excitement of the wide-eyed audience where
he was the oldest by far.

He had avoided books by Soviet authors because he did not
accept Socialist Realism as a genre. But now he asked me to
recommend what to read and checked out my recommendations
from the library to keep pace with me.

We spent our evenings talking. I gushed about the freedom and
promise of the post-Stalin era – the future belongs to me, as I put
it. But Leib generated doubts I did not want to have.

SLIDE 70 – Khrushchev

LEIB: Khrushchev is not giving us freedom. People are born free;
freedom cannot be given. But at times you have to lock it away

inside you. Do you know what cannot be locked away?
Menschlichkeit -- being a *mensch*.

SLIDE 71 – Lenin and Stalin

BENA: I agreed with him that Stalin was a criminal but insisted
that Lenin was a saint.

LEIB: My dear, Lenin was a political prostitute, a person without
conscience. He invented concentration camps and he was a
murderer!

BENA: I gasped at such sacrilege. But Leib would not relent and
was determined to set me straight. Hidden behind bookshelves
were Musya's pre-Revolution newspapers and magazines.

He placed a stack in front of me. And he placed two encyclopedias
in front of me – one from before the Revolution and the other a
Soviet edition. In the old one, it mentioned that Russia had lost a
particular war. In the Soviet one it mentioned that Russia had won
that same war.

LEIB: Russia lost that war. Nothing built on lies is justifiable or
ends well. To remain a mensch, you must think and understand;
And to survive you must keep quiet and stay away.

BENA: He watched me pore through these materials. When I
came up for air, I was disoriented and jolted out of my teenage
cocoon.

SLIDE 72 – Leib, 1959

LEIB: After what you have learned, would you want to have a

friend like Lenin? So, why would you allow him to define you? And even in this "Thaw," you can still be arrested for reading, writing or speaking out.

BENA: Leib possessed a breathtaking knowledge of Russian and Soviet history and a vast and unforgiving memory. Before our many visits, I prepared arguments to counter his reasoning and each time he quashed them without seemingly trying to and without raising his voice.

LEIB: Have you listened to the words of the songs you are taught?

"Bravely we'll go to battle for Soviet rule and, all as one, will die in the struggle for it." Suppose we all do die? And then what?

BENA: With Leib it was not a matter of proving his case in a quarrel; it was a matter of resetting my brain, wiring it to recognize logic. Everything was simple; all I needed to do was -- think.

SLIDE 73 – Leib's English grammar book and an *avoska*

Leib's dream project for retirement was adding English to his cache of languages. He acquired a thick grammar textbook, an unwieldy Russian-English dictionary, a two-volume English-Russian dictionary, and began with Shakespeare.

Four years later when he read and understood the Bard easily, he placed the grammar book and the dictionaries into a capacious *avoska* and handed it to me as I was packing for my return trip home one summer. He suddenly decided that it was useless at his age to learn a new language.

LEIB: I cannot throw out books. You do what you want with them.

BENA: I could not throw out books, either. Instead I began learning English, not with Shakespeare but modestly, with the basics. I still have the grammar book.

SLIDE 74 – Bena and Leib with Bena's daughters Emily and Polina

As the 1970s began, emigration became the leading topic of conversation in our family as it was for many others. My parents, my husband and I with our two daughters were going to apply to get out. Even though he was not well, Leib planned to emigrate with us and take Katya, his late wife's sister, with him as a wife so as not to leave her behind all alone.

He spent our last summer in the Soviet Union with us in Kiev. He loved opening the newspaper, pointing to different places and repeating,

LEIB: Lie, lie, lie. One doesn't have to read it to know that everything our government reports is a lie.

BENA: He could not have cheered our decision to emigrate more had I been his daughter.

LEIB: It will take time but you will eventually be a different person. Don't resist it.

SLIDE 75 – Leib, 1975

BENA: As the time was approaching to apply for permission

to emigrate, the pain Leib had been living with became severe. Various medical luminaries could not come up with a diagnosis.

Finally, he told me to proceed without him. I offered to wait, and for the first time his grumble was filled with tears...

LEIB: Please leave! I'm 75; it doesn't matter where I die. You have young children. If you get stuck, I will never forgive myself. Leave, leave, leave!

BENA: Six weeks after my family emigrated from the Soviet Union in 1976, Leib died of cancer of the liver.

SLIDE 76 – Leib

LEIB: *(Walking slowly towards the suitcase placed downstage, he recites "The Russian Mind," by Vyacheslav Ivanovich Ivanov, translator unknown. See page 2. His photo stays up throughout the poem. Music underscores the poem.)*

Willful and avid,
The Russian mind is dangerous as flame:
So unrestrainable, so clear,
A happy and a gloomy mind.

Like the steady hand of a compass
It sees the pole through swells and fog;
It leads the timid will
From distracted dreams to life.

Like an eagle gazing through the mist
To survey the valley's dust
It soberly contemplates the earth,
Floating in a mystic night.

(When he finishes, he places the costume accessories he removed from the coat tree into the suitcase)

SCENE 8

SLIDE 77 – Polina

(As Bena introduces her, Polina moves to one of the two coat trees and puts on her costume accessories.)

BENA: There remains one more child of Velvel and Sheina-Gitel, my beloved Grandmother Polina.

Her given name was Tsiporah but she was Tsipa to her parents. She disliked that nickname. In Russian, it resembled Tsip-Tsip-Tsip, the sound used to get a chicken's attention. She insisted on being called Pearl. Later on when living in Kiev, Pearl morphed into its most common Russian equivalent Polina.

SLIDE 78 – Portrait of Polina in Bena's office

This portrait of her hangs in my office at home. She talks to me all the time.

I grew up with Polina and lived both with her and near her until she died in 1972 when I was in my late twenties. She was precious.

Rebellion appealed to her: out with arranged marriages, with uneducated women, with men praying and making children they could not feed!

However, the new socialist path to universal happiness did not add up to common sense for her like it did for many other Jews, including some on other branches of my family tree. She catastrophized the times she lived in and felt quite alone in her assessment.

The Bolshevik Revolution may have elevated the Jews to equality with workers and peasants but at the price of Jewish tradition – what was there to crow about?

POLINA: After Mameh taught me to read, I spent my childhood as a gofer and nanny, sadly as I witnessed the death of nine of my little siblings whom I helped care for.

During Tateh's lessons with his students, I hovered nearby under the guise of any chore that allowed me to eavesdrop. Some of the comments I allowed to escape from my mouth shocked Tateh into admitting that, for a girl, I grasped the subject deeper than many of his pupils; maybe even as deeply as Avrum had grasped it at my age.

His praise raised my hope that he would bend his no-schooling-for-girls rule. Without seeking approval, Mameh enrolled me in a Jewish elementary school for girls. I attended it for only one day though before Tateh pulled me out:

BENA: "A girl does not need education! The household needs help."

POLINA: Neither my tears nor Mameh's entreaties softened Tateh's stance. Fortunately, my younger sisters Dinah and Esther got to attend school and Tateh could do nothing about it.

SLIDE 79 – Polina's sewing machine

When I was 7, as my older sister Khanah became engrossed in groom selection, I took over most of the housecleaning too. I soon began experimenting with recipes that had gone unchallenged for generations. And I volunteered to darn, knit, needlepoint and mend.

BENA: Her creative eye, nimble fingers and efficiency were so important to the family that Sheina-Gitel invested in a used hand-driven sewing machine with fancy gilt lettering "Singer 1873." That machine obeyed Polina for 60 some years until spare parts could no longer be found.

SLIDE 80 – The dress and robe Polina made for Rakhil and Bena

She considered the dress she made for my mother Rakhil around 1960 for some extra-special occasion and the house robe she made for me for my 25th birthday in 1970 as her crowning achievements.

SLIDE 81 – Bena Gnoyensky, Polina's husband

When a 20-year-old gentleman named Bena from the town of Korsun graduated from Yeshiva, his first order of the day was to find a bride. His older sister who had married a watchmaker from Belaya Tserkov, recommended going there and consulting Velvel.

I love this story.

POLINA: Bena arrived at our house on a Friday afternoon. I was barefoot, washing the stoop with a rag, the last task in pre-Sabbath cleaning.

Unbeknownst to me, Bena stared at my heavy braid that rested along my spine as I was scrubbing the steps. With the front hem of my skirt tucked into the waistband, my calves were visible. When

I was done, Bena bowed respectfully in an attempt to cover his staring and entered the house.

I later confessed that I had fallen in love with Bena then and there but had quashed the feeling because I was only 13 and took him for just another of Tateh's visitors, possibly already married.

Instead of asking to go through the formalities of a *shidduch*, Bena right away asked Tateh for my hand; me — the beautiful girl with a long braid who had just finished washing the stoop. He did not mention the bare legs, Polina always noted with a mischievous smile.

Tateh chastised Bena, an unmarried boy, for soliciting a *shidduch* without his father present. And anyway, I could not consent to marriage until I was 18. Bena told Tateh:

BENA: "My parents were married at her age but if that is the custom in your family, I will wait."

Velvel did not invite the disrespectful boy to share the Sabbath meal with the family. But Bena stayed in Belaya Tserkov. He kept books for several small businesses and eventually attended every Sabbath meal at Velvel's house.

POLINA: He sought my unchaperoned company, something Tateh specifically forbade. Dinah, Leib and Esther served sentry duty for our forbidden encounters, which were brief but long enough to slip in a kiss.

SLIDE 82 – A bedcover similar to one Khanah gave to Polina as a wedding present

In 1911, we did get married. By then, Bena had saved up enough to put an advance on a two-room house.

For the wedding, I wore those shoes Khanah gave me when she moved away. Escorted by her beloved Khaim wearing a top hat, she showed up at the nuptials with a swanky plush bedcover for us -- proof that I had married well.

BENA: Polina had much to brag about in her letters to her brother Avrum in Philadelphia.

SLIDE 83 -- Polina and Bena's wedding photo

POLINA: "My marriage is not an arranged one but was made for love. I married into a learned and well-to-do family. But I will not let Bena take a Rabbi position and force me to accept a passé role of *rabbetzin*. And I made my own wedding dress from new, never used before material."

BENA: Polina distinguished herself in Belaya Tserkov as avant-garde in two categories: as the first Jewish bride to do away with a traditional white gown in favor of a regular dress and as the first Jewish wife not to cover her hair with a *tichel* but to simply coil her braid around her head.

Polina sent Avrum her wedding picture. Avrum's daughter gave me that photo 70 years later. A note on the back says, "Aunt Pearl."

SLIDE 84 – Rakhil as a toddler, 1913

They named their first child -- my mother -- Rakhil.

Bena ended up a bookkeeper and, in a concession from Polina, a *kazyonny ravvin* -- a part-time Government Rabbi -- for the Empire registering marriages, births, etc.

SLIDE 85 – A synagogue destroyed in a pogrom in 1919

Another round of pogroms in 1919 drove Bena's parents out of their *shtetl* and into Kharkov, then the capital of Ukraine, where his siblings had moved earlier. Bena considered having us move there to be near them but….

POLINA: I refused to leave my parents. Even so, since he was not receiving letters from his family, Bena decided to travel to Kharkov to check up on his pregnant sister. He planned to return home in time for the birth of our next baby. After a seven year wait, I was finally pregnant again.

SLIDE 86 – Typhus illustration

BENA: The grubby cattle trains that transported people also transported germs. Bena was already sick with typhus when he arrived at his sister's home. And in a short time, he was gone. He was 35. He was buried in a mass grave.

POLINA: I gave birth to a boy before I knew that Bena had died. Had I known I would have named the baby Bena. But instead I named the baby Shmul, after my brother Yankel-Shmul – Kutsya -- who had died from the vinegar.

BENA: Shmul lived one month. Polina was also suffering from typhus. Delirious and burning with fever, she was so ill that she did not know that both her husband and infant son had died.

She was not expected to survive. Kutsya's widow, Khaya, buried the infant and miraculously nursed Polina back to life.

When Polina was told what had happened, she screamed so loud and so long that Khaya feared her veins would burst. As soon as she could function again, Polina moved back in with her parents. She brought only a few bundles of clothing with her but left the house she and Bena had lived in unlocked, never to return.

SLIDE 87 – Bena as a toddler, 1947

I was named after my grandfather Bena and I often heard from Polina that when I was born…

POLINA: *Gott* (God) has rewarded me more than I could dare to ask for by letting me utter the name Bena thousands of times.

BENA: It did not matter that Bena was a man's name because it was the only name for her grandchild -- boy or girl.

SLIDE 88 – Polina, 1911

In the marriage market following the typhus epidemic, Polina was a catch: 28 years old; only one child; the bonus of *yikhes* — lineage; beauty; and substantial housekeeping talents. She had her pick among the many proposals that came her way. And she had the same answer for each contender:

POLINA: There can be no one like Bena and I don't want anybody different.

BENA: She was so sought after that marriage proposals continued until Polina was in her 60s. On one of the last occasions, I was amused by Polina's response.

POLINA: He must have been *meshugge* to hope that I would leave you, my only grandchild, to wash a man's underpants.

SLIDE 89 – Typical room in a communal apartment

After her mother died in 1932, Polina went to live in Kiev in a single room of a communal apartment that housed a dozen families.

POLINA: Your mother and I lived in a 100-square-foot windowless room off the kitchen. One of the other residents of our communal apartment was a prostitute. There was one in your Uncle Leib's apartment in Leningrad as well. The government thought that the neighbors would reform their characters.

BENA: A few years later in June of 1941, Hitler invaded the Soviet Union. Those who thought about evacuating east had just a few weeks to get out of Kiev.

POLINA: I was inclined to stay and guard our room from being snatched up. But your mother insisted and I finally agreed to evacuate. Thus, we avoided the Nazi massacre at Babi Yar. We left Kiev in the nick of time. I carried my sewing machine, thread bobbins, some fabric and a supply of elastic for our underwear.

SLIDE 90 – An outdoor market in Siberia

BENA: After some miserable interludes in tiny, barely civilized towns they settled in Barnaul, a regional Center in southwest Siberia. The lady who rented them a room had never seen Jews before, though she knew enough to dislike them:

POLINA: "What! No horns?"

BENA: To keep from starving, they depended, to a large degree, on creative bartering of food rations and belongings at flea markets. The market in Barnaul grew at the beginning of the war along with the city.

POLINA: We had nothing to trade for food. As a working adult, your mother was eligible for a full ration of rye dough. But one day, the factory where she worked replaced some of the dough with pure alcohol. That's when my mother's entrepreneurial gene came alive in me. She sold *tichels*. I sold alcohol.

At the market, the little jars of alcohol flew out of my hands, despite the exorbitant price of two large potatoes for each. Most buyers drank down the jars right in front of me grunting with pleasure and respectfully gave me the empty jars back.

With part of the proceeds, I bought wide skirts from local women, opened them at the seams, pressed them with my landlady's iron and whipped out child-size skirts and dresses that proved as popular with women as the alcohol was with men.

But I was careful not to grow our little enterprise, not to show up too often or with large quantities or at the same spot or at regular intervals. Being an entrepreneur could lead to trouble, bringing charges of capitalist exploitation and in war time, even treason.

Yet we lived opulently relatively speaking. No more grumbling stomachs for us!

SLIDE 91 – Bena's parents Rakhil and Avram, Polina and Bena

BENA: After the war, they returned to Kiev where my mother married my father whom she'd known for a long time. Polina lived with us.

As I was growing up, Polina watched me do my homework; attempted and failed to improve my sprawling handwriting; directed my home rehearsals for school recitals; and listened to me.

Polina governed with few rules: Breakfast --a big affair of yesterday's dinner leftovers with bread with butter – was the law of the land. As was no-snack-between-meals. Soup was the gateway to any dinner.

SLIDE 92 – Bena at various ages and Polina

She could not teach me the Jewish dietary laws and run the risk that I might tell others that we kept kosher, meaning that we were religious. Even so she wanted me to observe them in a limited way even under false pretenses:

POLINA: Do not drink milk after eating meat. It will give you a stomachache.

BENA: Once, I washed down a meat patty with some milk, which was the only beverage available at that café. My stomach did not hurt but Polina groaned:

POLINA: *Vey is mir. (*Woe is me*).*

BENA: In 1960, Polina suffered a heart attack and was told to remain on her back for a month. While she was recovering, I untangled her hair, strand by strand and read to her. We began with *Uncle Tom's Cabin* which she took to right away even asking me to repeat some chapters. We both memorized large chunks of the novel. Polina recovered.

In her late 70s, Polina began suffering from recurring pneumonia that left her weak and pale and left me scared.

Our communal neighbor always kept the kitchen window open and cooked wearing a quilted coat and felt boots. She refused to close the window even in the winter when Polina was in the kitchen.

"Jews are weaklings!" she shouted.

I hissed back at her, my nose an inch from her face "If my Bábushka gets sick again, I'll kill you." This wiry peasant woman could have knocked me down in a flash, but incredibly, she gave in and closed the window.

SLIDE 93 – Bena's wedding to Mikhail (Dima)

By the time I got married, we had a large two-room private apartment. My husband, Dima, moved in with us. Our living arrangement changed when Dima managed to join a new thing called "Co-op." We built a small two-room private apartment and then swapped it with my parents. Polina would have preferred to stay with Dima and me.

But she had to live with my parents. Dima and I were at work all day and Polina was not well. My parents had retired by then and were able to care for her. For the last six months of her life and for the first time in her life, she had her own private room.
As Polina was leaving the old apartment for the last time, she whispered in my ear:

SLIDE 94 – Portrait of Polina in Bena's office

POLINA: "Don't be upset. I'm always here. Even after I'm not here."

SLIDE 95 – Rakhil, Polina's daughter, with Ruth, Avrum's daughter

BENA: Throughout her life, reading, storytelling and letter-writing were Polina's passions. She was the only one of her siblings to write to Avrum in Philadelphia. She encouraged my mother to keep in touch with Avrum's daughter Ruth.

My mother kept a greeting card from Ruth for a long time. But beginning in the early 1930s having a relative abroad served as evidence of spying. So my mother had to burn the card and Polina broke off her correspondence with Avrum.

SLIDE 96 – Polina, 1967

Polina's brother Leib in Leningrad was her soul mate. They

devoted pages to philosophical observations and discussions of word meanings. Leib lamented the absence of Yiddish publications in the Soviet Union as every one of Polina's letters, in his opinion, was a publisher-ready short story or essay.

Like her father Velvel had prodded her, Polina prodded me as I was growing up:

POLINA: Think, my child…. Suppose you prevail?

BENA: In due course, I realized that she had wanted me to answer, "And then what?" to myself before I acted.

In conversation, Polina was quick at coming up with succinct observations worthy to stand next to her father's. Looking back, countless subliminal messages must have flown by me unnoticed until some hit the mark later leaving an indelible impression on me.

POLINA: "Better not to wear tight clothes, let the boys guess, it's their job. Boys may look at you more if you wear tight clothes but how will you know what they think?"

BENA: "If you must do something, enjoy it, otherwise you'll lead a miserable life."

POLINA: "In fateful moments, you're responsible for your children, not your parents – the children are the future."

BENA: "When you give your children the last crust of bread, let them believe that you are not hungry. Mentioning sacrifice will make them feel guilty."

POLINA: "Ask for a tad more than you actually want so that when you get less – and people always get less – it will be exactly what you wanted."

BENA: And I especially remember her saying to me when as a teenager, I expressed doubt that old people knew anything....

POLINA: "If people know nothing when they get old, then you too will know nothing when you are old."

BENA: *(to Polina with gratitude)* I used this logic on my teenage children – it worked.

SLIDE 97 – Polina's grave site

Polina died at home in 1972. She was a month short of her 82nd birthday. Several hours before she died, Polina was playing "five-hundred-one" with my parents, a card game for three. They played every day. She interrupted the game to pick up the phone and call me with a reminder to put away the summer clothes for the winter.

Several days earlier, she had handed me and my daughter Emily the traditional Chanukah *gelt* in her usual amount of 72 kopeks. I knew what *gelt* meant — money — but not what Chanukah meant.

SLIDE 98 – Polina

(Polina walks slowly towards the suitcase placed downstage. The siblings take turns reciting a line from "The Unfinished Sewing" by Evdokiya Rostopchina, translator unknown. See page 2.)

(Her photo stays up throughout the poem. Music underscores the poem.)

KHANAH: The hour when woman sews her modest seam

DINAH: Brings silence, peace, and space for sweet reflection;

ESTHER: Far from the worldly crowd, she's sunk in contemplation;

AVRUM: Then she may read her soul, may gaze upon herself.

KUTSYA: Full work-table to hand, she sits,

LEIB: And stitches rapidly, absorbed in what she sews.

(Polina places her costume accessories she removed from the coat tree into the suitcase.)

SCENE 9

SLIDE 99 – The Pioneers

(Bena goes to one of the two coat trees and, with Polina's reluctant help, puts on a red neck scarf and the white pinafore.)

BENA: When Soviet children turned 9 years old, they took seriously the right -- rather the obligation -- to join the Pioneer organization and, thus, become Lenin's grandchildren. When I became a Pioneer, I was trusted to open the festivities by reciting the sacred Communist anthem, "The Internationale".

Like my Great-Uncle Leib later, Polina did all she could to prevent the Soviet mindset from taking hold in me. She tensed when she heard me practicing the words of the anthem.

SLIDE 100 – "The Internationale"

(Recites passionately in Russian only if the actor is fluent in Russian)

Вставай, проклятьем заклеймённый,
Весь мир голодных и рабов!
Кипит наш разум возмущённый

И в смертный бой вести готов. Весь мир насилья мы разрушим
До основанья, а затем Мы наш, мы новый мир построим, —
Кто был ничем, тот станет всем.

(Recites passionately in English.)

"We'll demolish the world of oppression completely
then we'll build our own new world in its place.

Who was a nothing will become an everything."

POLINA: What do you mean demolish the world of oppression?
One must first salvage what's usable. Or how will you know how
to build a new world? And remember that when a servant
becomes an overseer, no good will come of it.

Let's suppose all this happens – *und vus veiter?* And then what?
Trakht, mein kind. Think, my child.

SLIDE 101 – A photo of Young Pioneers marching

BENA: I arrived home from the festivities, flushed with pride,
wearing my red neck scarf and the Pioneer pin on the wing of my
pinafore. I announced:

"Now I'm a true Lenin's granddaughter."

SLIDE 102 – Bena's grandfathers

POLINA: *(hugging Bena from behind but bewildered at Bena's absence
of logic)* Lenin's granddaughter? Why Lenin's? You had two
wonderful grandfathers.
  (sternly)
Think my child. Suppose you prevail.

ENSEMBLE: *(stands)* And then what?

*(Long pause during which Bena walks to the suitcase and takes off the
red neck scarf and the pinafore. She kneels by the suitcase holding the
neck scarf and pinafore. She contemplates whether to take it with her to
Chicago or leave it. She decides to take it and closes the suitcase*

decisively and picks it up. She walks to the front of her desk and sits on the suitcase.)

SLIDE 103 – Bena's exit visa from the Soviet Union

BENA: My name is Bena. I was born in Chicago in 1976 when I was 31 years old.

SLIDE 104 – Bena's family in Chicago

On September 15, of that year, I arrived in my new country with Dima, his mother and our two daughters, Emily and Polina. My parents arrived the next year. We were seven of the hundreds of thousands of Soviet Jews who were saved in those years thanks to the "Save Soviet Jewry" movement.

When we got off the plane, a Mr. Vainer from the Hebrew Immigrant Aid Society met us.

A hearty "Welcome to Chicago!" exhausted his Russian vocabulary.

"Sprechst du Yiddish? Do you speak Yiddish?" he asked.
"Yo avode. Yes, of course" we replied much to his relief.

SLIDE 105 – Bena's first Chicago apartment

He drove us to the corner of West Morse Avenue and North Ashland Avenue in East Rogers Park. He pointed to a four-story building and gave us a key to a one-bedroom furnished apartment on the second floor where Jewish Family and Community Services had delivered two brand-new mattresses as a gift.

We signed for a $10 bill he produced. On a scrap of paper, he scribbled: "Tomorrow, 9 a.m., go to the JFCS office, 2710 West Devon Avenue."

SLIDE 106 – Free Soviet Jewry rally

Fist in the air, he proclaimed:
"*Gehen sie in drerd*! Let the earth swallow them!" Meaning the Soviet Union.

"*Sei gesund. Sei mazeldic.* Be well. Be fortunate," he added and was gone.
  (Smiles broadly as she stands holding the suitcase)
And then what?

(Ensemble forms a semi-circle behind Bena with Polina in the middle. They begin to hum quietly "There Was a Birch Tree in the Field.")

SLIDE 107 – Bena's graduation, 1985

Dima and I both secured good jobs eventually. We sponsored other immigrants. Dima passed away in 2002.

SLIDE 108 – Bena's children with their husbands and her grandchildren

Our daughters married. I have five grandchildren –
the great-great-great grandchildren of Velvel and Sheina-Gitel.

For 11 years following my mother's death in 2004, I researched and wrote my family story, meeting and keeping in touch with my cousins – the descendants of Avrum, Dinah and Esther Averbukh and of other branches of my tree; those in the U.S. in

Israel, in Germany and those who stayed behind in Russia and Ukraine.

SLIDE 109 – Home page of Bena's website

With help from many people and travels to the old country, I created this website. It contains my *yerushe* – my inheritance, my legacy and my possession to pass on to the new branches on our tree that are growing and are yet to grow.

(Bena starts to exit. She stops and turns when Polina speaks. Slow blackout)

POLINA: For some, the apple does not fall far from the tree. But it really does not fall at all -- because you belong to a family. You don't ever need to see them, you don't even need to know them, you are always part of that family.

(Bena blows a kiss to the Ensemble and exits.)

END OF PLAY

How Many Bushels Am I Worth?

How Many Bushels Am I Worth? ©

A play
by Bena Shklyanoy and Kevin Olson

based on Bena Shklyanoy's story of her family at
https://appledoesnotfall.com/

CHARACTERS
Bena – A younger woman
Alex – A younger man playing many characters

The play takes place mostly in Kiev and spans the years 1945 - present time. The setting should be suggestive not literal; perhaps a few crates that are rearranged for each scene to suggest a location, furniture or even a relationship. In the original production, there were stalks of wheat wrapped in burlap sacks around the set as well.

Bena should be costumed in attractive but plain and somewhat old-fashioned, drab and darkish clothing. Alex should be costumed in timeless business casual clothing.

Along the rear is a screen onto which will be projected key dates of events within each scene, animations, and/or slides. Each production will decide if and how they want to project images. In the original production, animations created by Clara Tomaz captured a key moment from the previous scene. These animations along with music connect one scene to the next.

SCENE 1

BENA: *(present time)* I was born in Chicago when I was 31 years old. Over the years people asked us how we made the decision to leave the Soviet Union and what hurdles we had to overcome. The simple answer we realized many years later was that it was not one specific event but rather all the tiny little events of day-to- day life that cumulatively brought us to the point where emigration was our life-jacket.

It was an agonizing decision to make and an agonizing process to go through. We knew that at any moment -- no matter how far along we were -- it could all fall apart.

As refuseniks then, we would have no jobs, fewer friends, and even more fear. Only the distance of so much time helped me understand how the realities I encountered as a child, teen, wife and mother motivated the decision to grab our children and run.

(Bena exits.)

(In the original production, a short series of slides accompanied by music was shown here. They provided an overview of both life in the Soviet Union as well as depicted key moments in the play such as women crowding about bras for sale in a department store.)

SCENE 2

ALEX: *(entering)* A Jew walks into the Soviet Union's Department of Visas:
> *(gruffly as the worker in the office)*
"Why did you apply to emigrate?"

"Two reasons. One: my neighbor promised to kill me when the Soviet regime is over."

"The Soviet regime will never be over."

"That's the second reason."

> ### Project: JULY 29, 1945. Kiev, Ukraine, Union of Soviet Socialist Republics

Bena was born in Kiev.

Bena's mother - Rakhil - had an easy pregnancy and a quick delivery. No matter if the baby was a boy or a girl, the name was carved in stone: Bena, after Rakhil's father. Since circumcision was outlawed....

BENA: *(enters and plays this scene as a 3-year old girl)* My parents are happy I am a girl.

ALEX: She was an only child, but she was hardly alone. The first year of her life she lived, with her parents, Avram and Rakhil, her Bábushka Polina and Avram's four sisters and their families in three connecting rooms.

BENA: *(proudly)* 750 square feet.

ALEX: The building was under the jurisdiction of the MVD —
Ministry of Internal Affairs — a KGB-like organization where
Avram worked as the head of bookkeeping.

At that time a family thanked fate for having 60 square feet to live
in, so three large rooms with only two other families sharing the
rest of the communal apartment spoke volumes of Avram's
position.

But when Bena showed symptoms of TB despite Rakhil's many
precautions, doctors recommended they move to a safer
environment. Move? That was laughable! As if they didn't know
that nobody had anywhere to go

BENA: Daddy thinks that his boss will not give us a new room.
     (She is impressed; in a tone: that guy could do anything!)
But his boss is a Colonel who had personally met Lenin!

ALEX: *(cynically)* A brothel is opening in Moscow and reliably
communist women are being sought to work there. The
requirement for being hired? Anyone who had met Lenin.

The Colonel admired Avram's professional ability and had even
invited him and Rakhil over to his 7-room private apartment. But,
still, a Jew and one who had chosen not to join the Communist
Party had better remember his place. So, Avram was reluctant to
ask for a new room.
     (with admiration)
But Rakhil sprang into action.

One early morning she darted past the guard stationed in front of
the building where the Colonel lived. Flying up the stairs to his

73

floor and past his wife, she found him still in bed. She talked fast
and later that day the Colonel assigned Avram a new room

BENA: *(interrupting, disappointed)* 140 square feet –

ALEX: …in another MVD-controlled building. They shared this
communal apartment with only one other family: a Lieutenant-
Colonel, his wife who worked as a typist at the MVD and doubled
as an informant, and…

BENA: *(happy to have a friend and interrupting again)* Lusya is two
years older than me!

ALEX: …their daughter. They were ordered to relinquish one of
their four rooms to Bena's family.

BENA: *(child repeating what she heard from grownups)* We share a
kitchen, a lavatory, a washroom with a sink and tub, and a foyer.
But we can't go into the washroom because the Lieutenant-
Colonel is mad at us for taking away their extra room.

ALEX: A unique Soviet phenomenon, communal apartments
democratically housed as many families as there were rooms;
rarely did a family have more than one room which functioned
as…

BENA: *(listing and giving a tour of their room)* living room,
bedroom, office, nursery.

ALEX: *(whispering so Bena does not hear)* …and hospice.
In some bathrooms, separate nails held a stack of newspaper
squares that belonged to the family whose name was scratched on
the wall. When real toilet tissue appeared on the scene, the lucky

owner of the precious roll brought it with him, or simply brought the requisite number of sheets…

BENA: (*a whisper shout; starts hopscotching*) Don't let them know you have real toilet paper!

ALEX: No wonder the Russian language does not have a word for privacy. Neighbors knew everything about each other, whether by observation, gossip, eavesdropping, or opening others' mail.

BENA: (*stops hopscotching.*) Lusya's mommy always listens outside our door. When we open our door, it sometimes hits her, and we apologize?
> (*Disappointed*)

Mommy, Daddy and Bábushka always talk in a language I don't understand so that Lusya's mommy – and I – won't know what they are saying.

ALEX: It was Yiddish.

BENA: (*barely lets him finish*) And they have funny nicknames for people they are talking about. And they keep staring at me, making the mouth-locking signal.
> (*Alex and Bena both make it; he looks sternly at her*)

When they speak Russian, they don't want to tell me what the words I don't already know mean. And when they do explain, they tell me not to ask questions.
> (*She recites as a child would.*)

Arrest means -- going away forever;
exile means -- the place where one goes away forever;
statute means -- the reason for going away forever;
execution means -- not breathing again forever.

I play house with Lusya in her room. I don't really like to play house. But if I do, she will let me look through *Krokodil* *(pronounced like Krokodeel, with stress on ee)*, a funny magazine her family has.

Lusya's daddy comes over to me and points to a drawing in the magazine of a man with a mustache in a uniform and another man with a double chin, a pipe in his mouth, and a stomach hanging to his knees. *(she giggles)*

ALEX: *(being sugary nice)* "Which man do you like more?"

BENA: *(In a tone "goes without saying.")* The funny fat man.

ALEX: *(with pride)* Bena was not yet 3 years old and already showed a preference for Churchill over Stalin!

The following day at work, the Personnel Department had a question for Avram:

"Is that what you teach your child?" -- meaning choosing Churchill over Stalin. Avram acknowledged "shortcomings" in raising his daughter and vowed to correct his mistakes.

BENA: *(child sharing grownups' admonition.)* I am never to go into Lusya's rooms and never to talk to her again. If I do, Mommy says Daddy will be arrested.

ALEX: The reaction to Avram's "shortcomings" was swift – an order came down to fire him forthwith for cosmopolitanism.

The campaign against "rootless cosmopolitans" was one of Stalin's last murderous campaigns. It mostly centered on Jews:

(as if reciting a slogan)
"the stateless vagrants of the world not capable of patriotism and loyalty to a single country."

BENA: *(angrily refuting what Alex said)* But the Colonel did not fire Daddy! He was not afraid to protect Daddy because he had personally met Lenin.

ALEX: Avram expected to be fired at any moment. One did not have the choice to resign.

BENA: *(clarifies)* You could only resign if you were arrested or executed.

Project: 1949

ALEX: Bena is about to turn 4.

BENA: *(sits down on the floor center stage. Starts softly then faster and more and more intense, breathlessly)* I am playing very quietly, like my parents told me, with my ball in the foyer of the apartment. The door to Lusya's dining room is open. I roll the ball too hard and it rolls all the way into it. They are eating. Lusya has red bows in her braids!

Her mother waves at me to come in to get the ball. I run to the door and stop. I can't lift my feet. If I go in, Daddy will be arrested and go away forever.

I can't breathe.

Lusya's mother walks over to the ball and kicks it back to me. I'm scared and I shriek. I'm dizzy as I pick up the ball.

Mommy picks me up and holds me tightly.
I start breathing again.

ALEX: *(pause)* These are Bena's first clear memories.

Animation for Scene 2 plays with music.

SCENE 3

Project: JANUARY 1951

ALEX: Bena is 5 1/2. The older she got the more she preferred to stay indoors. The outdoors was no fun.

Living reminders of the Great Patriotic War as the Soviets called World War II filled the streets: crutches, wooden shafts instead of shoes, empty pant legs pinned-up above the knee. Legless men on wheeled pallets swished around by pushing themselves with gloved fists. They were tarnishing the landscape of the victorious nation – the very sight of their stumps had a demoralizing effect.

One night, militia rounded up the homeless veterans, loaded them into cattle cars, and sent them to camps known as the "graveyards for war veterans." It was suggested that Kiev alone contributed several thousand victims that night.

BENA: *(plays scene as a 5-year old. Doesn't understand what she did wrong)* I get spanked for being happy they have vanished.

ALEX: The Colonel could no longer protect Avram's job; his clout ran its course — personal acquaintanceship with Lenin notwithstanding. He had to fire Avram. They had 72 hours to vacate their room. Non-MVD employees could not reside in that building.

BENA: I don't care. Daddy is only fired, not arrested. Bábushka and I stay with Mommy's friend in her 80-square-foot room. Mommy stays with another friend. And Daddy sleeps on a desk under the stairs in his old office building.

ALEX: The young soldier on duty, grateful for a past favor, let Avram in late at night for a few hours. If found out, both Avram and the soldier would have been executed.

After nine months, Avram finally secured a job.
A head of a manufacturing plant put his reputation and his freedom on the line to petition his superiors to authorize the hiring of a "cosmopolitan" who had been fired from MVD.

Shaken by Avram's story, he also assigned the family an apartment even before his superiors approved his request. The plant and the apartment were located on the outskirts of Kiev, in Kurenevka, a largely rural area near Babi Yar.

BENA: *(childishly oblivious)* I'm happy -- we are together again.

ALEX: A man of Stalin's age walks around Red Square carrying a poster that says:

"Thank you, Comrade Stalin, for my happy childhood!"

Someone says to the man, "Wait, when you were a child, Stalin was not yet our leader."

He replies, "That's why I'm thanking him!"

Joseph Stalin ruled the Soviet Union for almost 30 years. His campaigns against spies and enemies of the people destroyed farmers and much of the Soviet brainpower; entire ethnicities were deported to remote areas. Those passed over by his genocidal meat-grinder lived in constant fear that remained with them long after Stalin was gone.

Despite that, most Soviets, among them many of those persecuted and their families, worshipped Stalin, saw a protector in him, a godlike figure incapable of flawed judgment. They referred to him as the Father of All Nations.

Project: MARCH 5, 1953

Bena is in first grade on the day Joseph Stalin died.

BENA: *(takes a beat; watches her mother celebrate. Dumbfounded)* Mommy rushes into the house after work and, still in her wet galoshes, starts skipping around the table, clapping and chanting

ALEX: *(clapping and chanting)*
"Der Tateh iz geshtorben! Der Tateh iz geshtorben!
Dad has died! Dad has died!"

BENA: *(bewildered)* Bábushka looks to the ceiling and thanks God

ALEX: *(looking to ceiling, whispering loudly fervently)* "a danken Gott"

(gives her the mouth-locking signal. She follows suit)

BENA: Bábushka splurges—five eggs are nothing to sneeze at—on a small sponge cake.

(confused) But the radio is playing sad music.

At school my classmates sob and wipe their noses with their sleeves. Everybody wears a black band on their left arm except me. I am happy because of the special sponge cake. The teacher asks me:

ALEX: *(softly)* "Don't you know that Comrade Stalin died?"

BENA: *(naively)* I know somebody's Daddy is dead. Whose Daddy is it?

When I get home after school, I tell Mommy and Bábushka that I have to wear a black arm band to school for the next three days. Mommy says that the stores don't have any black fabric. And Bábushka says she has no scraps of black fabric.

ALEX: Bena always wondered if Bábushka, an accomplished seamstress, really did have some black fabric.

BENA: *(sighs)* I have to go to school without an arm band. We are also not allowed to smile for three days but I forget that and smile. A tattle-tale boy runs to our teacher:

ALEX: *(in a tattle-tale tone)* "Bena is smiling!"

Project: MARCH 20, 1953

Nikita Khrushchev became the next leader of the Soviet Union. Three years later he denounced the horrors of the Stalin era and exonerated Stalin's victims.

For a short time, Khrushchev relaxed the political and cultural climate and even encouraged publications that exposed Stalin's excesses of power. In an unintended consequence, this policy triggered the dissident movement.

BENA: They are taking down the portrait of Stalin in the foyer at school. And our principal announces that we now live in a free country.

ALEX: Still though when discussing Peter the Great in class one day, Bena's history teacher said: "Peter's appropriation of Swedish land was justified because Russia needed a window to Europe."

BENA: *(raising her hand, stands up when Alex motions her to)* "But that was not Russian land."

ALEX: "But Russia needed a window to Europe."

BENA: "But that was not Russian land." The teacher orders me to sit down and later calls Dad at work to tell him that my big mouth will put the family in danger. When I get home everyone pounces on me, terrified. Bábushka cries.

ALEX: "One must understand and one must keep mum."

BENA: She then makes the mouth-locking signal and goes to the headrest of her sofa and pulls out three books. Their pages are yellow, the binders are frayed.

ALEX: *(nodding and speaking wistfully)* "Ah, Sholom Aleichem...."

BENA: *(surprised)* Dad is turning the pages strangely from left to right. The alphabet looks strange too. It must be Yiddish!

"Please teach me how to read Yiddish."

ALEX: *(firmly but giving in)* "That is not safe. But if you promise not to tell anyone, I will read you the stories out loud." Avram read and re-read the stories to her every evening for two years.
    (Pause)

Project: EARLY 1960s

Having retired and not scared any longer about losing his job, Avram with much trepidation started ordering matzah for Passover. That was an elaborate annual process whose first step was establishing the correct date for the holiday.

BENA: Dad doesn't want to enter the synagogue to ask because it would get us in trouble. He wanders around near the synagogue looking for older Jewish-looking men.

ALEX: He whispers to each one in Yiddish:

"When does Passover start? When will the synagogue begin accepting orders for matzah?" Some pretend not to hear or understand. But eventually one will reply furtively.

BENA: He has to sneak around to the back door of the synagogue to place his order and pay for it.

ALEX: The final step is picking up the order.

BENA: "Can I go with you?"

ALEX: *(horrified)* "God forbid! Promise that you will never come near the synagogue. Stay at least a block away or you'll be photographed. You'll be thrown out of school. You can lose your job."

BENA: I don't even know where the synagogue is!

ALEX: On pickup day, Avram leaves the house at dawn carrying two suitcases with a pillowcase in each. He will take a roundabout

way to the synagogue and an even wider roundabout way home with the matzos hidden inside the pillowcases.
(Pause. Tongue-in-cheek)
"Next year in Jerusalem" -- indeed.

Teaching Hebrew was all but outlawed in the Soviet Union. And If revealing one's Jewish traditions was dangerous, ironically covering up one's Jewish background was also a serious offense. It was an indication that the person did not believe in

BENA: *(ironically)* "The Friendship of all Peoples" – a pillar of Communism.

Animation for Scene 3 plays with music.

SCENE 4

BENA: *(present time)* Sometime after we arrived in Chicago, the caseworker at Jewish Family Service arranged for us to attend a full-fledged Passover Seder at a volunteer's house.

To say that we felt out of place there was an understatement. We clustered around the grandmother who spoke Yiddish. And were flattered that she flew in from Florida to meet us.

The harmony did not last however. The grandmother went on about how <u>her</u> illiterate parents had reached America's shores with nothing but the clothes on their backs.

Whereas we, professionals, even doctors and engineers, were fleecing American Jewry! We had to laugh! No one was lower on the Soviet social ladder or pay scale than doctors and engineers!

Americans assumed that professionals had to be valued. We did not yet comprehend that professionals could be valued.

The Seder dragged on forever. Emily and Polina kept asking for food, thankfully in Russian. They were asked to find the afikomen and we had no idea what that was.

The lady of the house was insulted by our ignorance.

SCENE 5

ALEX: Khrushchev comes back from the U.S., all fired up about catching up with and surpassing America in every possible category, from milk to bombs. He calls in his assistant and says:

"America has a thousand synagogues and we only have 20. Catch up and surpass! You have a month."

A month later the assistant reports: "No problems with synagogues, we have over a thousand now. The issue is finding rabbis. People who apply are not Party members.
        (horrified)
Some are even Jewish."

Project: 1961

In 1961, Bena turns 16.

BENA: *(as a 16-year old with pride and teenage excitement)* I get my passport.
        (matter-of-factly)
The fifth line on it states my nationality: Jewish. Of course: both my parents are Jewish.

ALEX: With dozens of nationalities in the Soviet Union, the expression "fifth line" applied exclusively to Jews.

BENA: A Yellow Star worn on identification instead of on clothes.

ALEX: Also that year, the Party earmarked 1980 as the year when the transition from mere socialism to pure communism would be complete.

(delivers joke's first line as if a teacher asking a question)
"Why do we have to be hungry if we are on the way to pure communism?

BENA: *(with teenage exasperation)* "Because eating on the road will slow us down. We'll eat when we get there."
(sighs)
Food is always *deficete*, everything is *deficete*.
(deficete: stress on the last syllable, like in compete)

ALEX: *Deficete* -- "not available" or "in short supply." Queues form in minutes fueled by rumors that some item would be available.

A man comes home and catches his wife with a lover. "Are you crazy? Why are you home when there is a line for oranges in the store next door?"

Shortages happened at random to random products and for random durations:

BENA: sugar, eggs, buckwheat, mayonnaise, shoes, buttons.

ALEX: Some shortages lasted for years, some for a short time. Someone said:
(speaks in an official Soviet tone)
"Soviet industry always does <u>not</u> produce something."

But shortages aside, the real obstacle to converting to pure Communism was the West. The malicious influence of Western music and fashion had to be contained. Teens were craving the depraved boogie-woogie, the Charleston, jazz, rock-n-roll. And everyone craved the superior imported clothes.

BENA: Soviet stuff is pitiful.

ALEX: Nothing could reduce the allure of foreign-made goods. And the vision of the glamorous forbidden world behind them was…titillating. Especially the vision of imported lingerie.

Pantyhose crossed the border from Czechoslovakia in the late 1960's and, for a long time, they were *deficete*. Bras made in the Soviet Union only came in three sizes.

BENA: I can only find imported bras for sale in the public bathroom on the main street, Kreshchatik. Frumpy women clutching roomy purses are selling them. I have to wait for one to whisper to me…

ALEX: *(whispers near Bena's ear, looking furtive)* "Czech underwear?" "German bra?"

A pair of underwear went for a day's wages. Not surprisingly: it passed through many channels, beginning with a sailor or a ballerina traveling internationally, before ending up in Kiev's public bathroom. It got so bad that the Minister of Culture, a female, stated in her speech at a top-level Party meeting:

ALEX AND BENA: "Every Soviet woman has the right to wear a quality bra."

ALEX: *(blat pronounced like blot)* Blat or "inside connections" was the backbone of the Soviet economy and of day-to-day life. One did not buy things. One "obtained" things paying with money, alcohol, a stick of salami, perfume, anything you had access to.

Project: 1962

Some of Bena's classmates were meeting regularly at her apartment studying for university entrance exams, dreaming and enjoying Bábushka's non-alcoholic cherry cordial.
(exchanging a knowing smile with Bena)
The Soviet Manischewitz.

BENA: These exams are stringent and there are always more applicants than available spots. How many Jews will they really accept, anyway?

ALEX: Her friends accuse her of fishing for compliments and bat away any suggestion that their country sanctions discrimination. To her though, anti-Semitism is an ever-present elephant in the room.

BENA: My heart is set on the six-year evening program in Russian language at the Kiev University.

ALEX: A school recognized as much for its quality of education as for its rabid Ukrainian nationalism and anti-Semitism.

BENA: But to apply to the evening program, I have to furnish employment verification and later demonstrate that I have prospects for getting a job in my intended field of study. Or I will be dismissed. A month before the entrance exams, the engineering department at my father's plant hires me to trace drawings.

ALEX: Bena was not anxious about the entrance exams.

BENA: *(matter-of-factly)* I expect to fail. I've known since childhood the deck is stacked against me.

ALEX: Yet, the first three exams go smoothly. Then comes the one in Russian literature. The professor pounces:

Do you agree with Yevtushenko's *Babi Yar* that anti-Semitism has a place in the Soviet Union? Should that poem have seen the light of day? Would you recite the work of other contemporary poets? Do you agree with Ehrenburg's anti-Stalin novel "The Thaw"?

BENA: I speak, quote, recite for almost an hour fueled by defiance and adrenaline and the recognition that I have nothing to lose. Apparently, I avoid the undertow — the interrogator states that though I deserve a "3" she'll generously give me a "4".
(Exuberant)
I get in!
(her mood changes quickly; impatiently)
But since I am majoring in humanities, tracing drawings will likely remain my lot in perpetuity. The 5th line on my passport won't let me get a job in my field of study.

ALEX: A virtual sign "Jews need not apply" protected ideological-front institutions like the media, schools, kindergartens, libraries and scientific firms from the Zionists.

BENA: *(official tone)* The leading enemy of progressive mankind.

ALEX: It was a given that the future did not look promising for the intelligentsia, meaning professionals, particularly the Jewish intelligentsia -

A teacher consoled a child whose father was a doctor: "That's OK, bad things happen."

BENA: During my first summer break, I spent a few days at a friend's house in Moscow. She tells me to begin with a pilgrimage to Lenin's Mausoleum. I go. But the queue that snakes around Red Square promises hours in the hot sun. What a waste of time!

ALEX: When Bena returns to work....

BENA: I foolishly admit to my Komsomol -- Young Communist League leader -- that I skipped the Mausoleum. He threatens to convene an emergency conference to assess my political leanings. I am petrified.

But as luck would have it, that night the janitor catches him in the attic with a woman not his wife. Whew...he now had worries other than my mausoleum transgression.

Project: 1964

ALEX: Suddenly, Khrushchev relinquished his throne supposedly because of ill health. Leonid Brezhnev set out to reverse the remnants of Khrushchev's liberal reforms.

BENA: I am so busy, I barely register our move to a new apartment. Now we live at a sought-after address:

ALEX: *(slightly sarcastic)* 14 Friendship of Peoples Blvd.
   (pause)
Rakhil's networking skills got Bena a job as a proofreader in an engineering firm that designs installations for boilers and burners. This job title qualified as work in her field of study and saved Bena from dismissal from the university.

BENA: And soon I get transferred to the newly established information department and am promoted from proofreader to translator.

ALEX: Bena had a flair for languages and was familiar with several. In her new job, she translated technical periodicals into Russian from European languages; compiled lists of recommended sources; and wrote brochures for seminars.

The pre-requisite to Bena's degree thesis defense was a course in Scientific Communism, a finishing touch to the ideological series of required courses on
     (talking quickly, counting on his fingers)
the History of the Communist Party, Political Economy, Scientific Atheism, and Marxist-Leninist Philosophy divided into dialectical materialism and historical materialism. But...

BENA: *(interrupting)* Do you know how the dialectical materialism class started?

(pompously) "Let me clarify the difference between materialism and dialectical materialism: a chicken is materialism, a given chicken is dialectical materialism."

ALEX: ...but scientific communism focused specifically on the current, and
     (raising his voice; index finger in the air as in 'pay attention')
"the inevitable final stage of capitalism's decay vis-à-vis the blossoming of socialism."

BENA: At least this professor knows we'll easily catch the hidden meaning, despite his poker face.

ALEX: *(tongue in cheek)* "Yes, capitalism will decay. It won't happen tomorrow, but capitalism is certainly
     (slowly; stretching the words)
decaying, decaying, decaying…"

ALEX AND BENA: *(laughing then looking up wistfully and savoring the smell of the forbidden)*
… but the smell is rather splendid."

Animation for Scene 5 plays with music.

SCENE 6

Project: 1967

ALEX: At home, Bena's family shares a phone line with a neighbor and with the intercom of a nearby hotel. The connections cross regularly. One such errant call brought a man into Bena's life.

BENA: A crossed connection repeatedly sends Dima to our line instead of to his boss' line.

ALEX: His formal name is Mikhail. But he goes by Dima.

BENA: This stranger keeps me on the phone, no matter how hard I try to finish the conversation. It doesn't work, even when I play the ace that has always stopped many an unwanted suitor: "I'm tall."

ALEX: "Good. So am I."

BENA: Bábushka tells me all the time that when I meet a man who loves me like her father loved her mother and like Dédushka Bena loved her and like my father loves my mother – I will know. After hanging up the phone this Sunday evening – do I know?

ALEX: Dima knew, he always insisted, the instant he heard Bena's voice.

BENA: He wheedles the apartment number out of me as well as a day and time to come over. It's highly unlikely he intends to show up.
(a beat or two with her waiting)

He is tall and balding, with a gray felt hat in one hand and a small bunch of wild flowers in the other. His gray eyes laugh as if holding in a joke. Four hours fly by.

We spent our first date braving March drizzle and slush. We try to get a table at a new café that looks as funky, they say, as cafes abroad. It even has some tables for two, but we must wait in a long queue. As we approach my building at the end of the evening Dima says – ooh, he looks so solemn:

ALEX: "When I left your house the evening we met I was too excited to take the trolley. I walked home and wondered if I would be able to give you the life you deserve."

BENA: Is this his way of asking me to marry him?

ALEX: Soviet society compelled women to marry early. A girl proved her respectability with modest clothes and manners, by not progressing beyond kisses, and by not admitting the need to pee, no matter how long the date.

Revolutionary doctrine taught that sexuality, though undeniable,
        (*Official Soviet tone*)
"represented a harmful appetite utilized by capitalists to control the working people."

The book *Twelve Sexual Commandments of the Revolutionary Proletariat* "stated that sexual intercourse must not repeat often." The word sex was never uttered.

BENA: Dima and I submit our marriage application at the all-the-rage Kiev Wedding Palace instead of the dreary office of vital statistics.

ALEX: Marriage presented a once-in-a-lifetime access to the special wedding store full of *deficete* sold at government prices and without standing in lines. The place was clean, the staff polite, the goods neatly displayed. No wonder people joked that the atmosphere tempted a customer to jump over the counter and ask for political asylum.

Project: SEPTEMBER 5, 1967

BENA: Our wedding party proceeds up the stairs and into a large hall. A woman in a white above-the-knee dress and an over-the-shoulder satin sash admonishes us to keep our union, the building block of the Soviet society, strong and unshakeable. We and our witnesses sign the register and we exchange rings. Then…

ALEX AND BENA: "in the name of the Union of Soviet Socialist Republics"

BENA: She pronounces us husband and wife. We are all celebrating back in our apartment. Suddenly my normally low-key father starts quietly singing the Yiddish wedding toast:

ALEX: *(singing)"Lo mir alle in eynem, lo mir alle in eynem, trinken a glezele vine."*

Animation for Scene 6 plays with music.

SCENE 7

Project: JUNE 2, 1968

ALEX: Their first child – a daughter is born. When Bena's contractions began, Dima flagged down a private car to take her to the hospital, there was no time to wait for an ambulance.

BENA: Twisting with pain I change into a hospital gown and start answering a lengthy questionnaire. I can't wait though.

ALEX: *(snaps)* "First-timers have no patience. Go find the delivery room."

BENA: I trudge down the agonizingly long hallways.

ALEX: The post-delivery room was packed. So they put Bena in the pre-delivery room where there was a vacant bed. The room was full of screaming, squealing, and moaning creatures writhing on twin beds. Soviet medicine did not believe in easing labor pain with medications. For the standard seven-day stay Bena was transferred to a room with two rows of twin beds, four in each row.

BENA: The infants swaddled mummy-like in flannel arrive on rolling pallets every three hours, from 6 in the morning to midnight. I will not see my daughter unswaddled until we bring her home.

ALEX: Three times a day the orderlies placed plates with cold food on nightstands. The cockroaches on them were apparently sterilized. Flowers or visitors were not permitted, for fear of germs. Bena talked to Dima through a small pane in the top part of the window.

BENA: Traditionally, the mother chooses the name for the firstborn. I have no close relatives who are deceased, so we agree on Mila, for Dima's father Moisey. The full name is Emilia.

ALEX: The week Mila was born, Dima received a promotion to head the construction department of his company. But the promotion had a string attached —

BENA: *(with disdain)* — obligatory Communist Party membership.

ALEX: Dima had hoped to dodge that string but had now run out of tricks.

BENA: Membership in my family and in the Party is mutually exclusive! Astonished by my stone-cold resolve, Dima sacrifices the job. He finds a job as a low-level engineer and is quickly promoted. The job pays much less. But I am happy and, to my relief, so is he.

Project: AUGUST 1968

ALEX: In August, the Soviet Union invaded Czechoslovakia for introducing liberal reforms known as the Prague Spring. The invasion was justified as "aiding a comrade in need."

BENA: *(softly and fearfully)* From Voice of America we learn that several Muscovites protested the invasion in Red Square. And that they are arrested or sent to psychiatric wards. They are daring to speak out. Precious few do. We feel beholden to them and are ashamed of our cowardice.

Animation for Scene 7 plays with music.

SCENE 8

BENA: *(present time)* In 1967, a year before the Prague Spring and 50 years after the Bolshevik Revolution, two things really shook up the USSR.

Stalin's daughter Svetlana Alliluyeva defected to the West and requested political asylum in the United States. She besmirched his memory in her tell-all book.

And the unthinkable happened! Israel defeated the invading Arab armies in the Six-Day War. The USSR threw a tantrum and severed diplomatic relations with Israel.

Anti-Semitic hysteria saturated the airwaves. Overnight, Israel transformed from a weakling to a Zionist warmonger. And Soviet Jews, from trapped pushovers to a people that had a home. Some people stopped talking to their Jewish colleagues and neighbors. The phrase "this is not your motherland, go to your Israel" accompanied bus rides and lines for food.

Dima and I felt strong and proud; an unfamiliar and quite addictive feeling. There-was no turning back. It didn't matter that we had to hide our pride or that we remained trapped.

We Soviet Jews discovered that Israel and even other countries wanted us.

In the dead of night, half-jammed Voice of America reports proved that the world is fighting for us and was even prepared to ransom us.

If the Soviet Union wanted American grain – and oh, did it want bushels and bushels of American grain! – it had to allow Jews to emigrate.

In private, we taunted our government:
        (with venom; gloating)
"Ah -- look who is trapped now! You don't think I'm worth much? Think again! My worth is measured in bushels."

SCENE 9

Project: 1969

ALEX: On a business trip to Moscow, Dima ran into a former classmate who had applied to emigrate to Israel. According to him, the Party had a new directive on the books to allow up to 1,500 Jews to emigrate each year.

BENA: The gnawing thought of emigration hunkers down in the back of our minds.

My parents drink in reports from the *Voice of America* and BBC like water in a desert. They also visit with soon-to-be emigrants to wish them luck and to gather information that we might use should we decide to get out.

The few Soviet Jews leaving the country kindle an unquenchable craving in us. Not that we can verbalize what the craving is for.

ALEX: A new joke made the rounds: A Jew approaches two other Jews on the street and says: "Whatever you are talking about, we have to get out."

BENA: Missives from emigrants to their families in the Soviet Union are our favorite genre of literature. We do not actually know anyone personally who emigrated. But the grapevine spreads the information from them in quiet conversations. We pick up important things to know about the journey out.

And we are getting more and more anxious. As a new saying goes "Cowards leave, risk-takers stay." And we are definitely cowards.

ALEX: Emigration was allowed only for the purpose of "family re-unification." So, to apply, one required an invitation from an Israeli relative – real or imaginary – usually imaginary. No one really cared as long as there was an invitation.

Further, to be allowed to apply for emigration, it was enough for just one family member to be Jewish.

Hence, the joke -- "a Jewish spouse is not a luxury…

BENA: …"but a means of transportation."

ALEX: Those who applied were subject to immediate "voluntary" loss of job, stripping of war medals, and contempt and boorishness at the Department of Visas and Registrations – O.V.I.R. -- and at every place that issued the documents needed known as *spravki*, written confirmations of facts.

Soviet Jews began giving their names and addresses to those who were emigrating. The Israeli government then made sure that invitations from "long-lost cousins" were issued.

BENA: Mom sets out to find willing and dependable messengers to trust with our names. She wants us to remain in the shadows. We cross our fingers.

Project: *AUGUST 1972*

ALEX: The Soviet Union adopts a new law. Simply stated: "If you leave, repay us for the education we gave you." Dubbed the Diploma Tax, the amount depended on the degree held and the schools attended.

BENA: 10,000 rubles for each of us. 20,000 rubles is as unattainable as a million. We backpedal on the requests to pass on our names. We are trapped.

(Long Pause)

Bábushka passes away.

(Pause. Takes time to recover)

We get some hope from the jammed radio stations which keep us abreast of America's response to the Diploma Tax. The greatest nation in the world rolls into action on our behalf!

Project: 1973

ALEX: And finally, the Soviet government buckled under the threat of losing trade benefits with the United States, especially losing American wheat. The diploma tax was revoked.

(Pause)

One day when Bena was picking Mila up at day care, Mila's face had traces of tears. Her group-mate had taken her doll but had said, "I did not take Mila's doll!"

The teacher calmed Mila down by saying that Lenin sat in the sky and saw everything and would mete out a just punishment to the other girl. On the way home, Mila was quite enthusiastic about Lenin taking care of her from the sky.

BENA: *(helplessly)* I can't tell Mila that Lenin is not all powerful in the sky! She will tell her teacher and we'll all pay the consequences. I have no choice but to become the teacher's accomplice. Argh.

ALEX: Dima's reaction to the story was instant: "We are getting out."

BENA: We resume passing out our names. And we must start preparing because when an invitation from Israel does arrive, the authorities might search our house, despite our insignificance.

So, we give away our subversive material, and an issue of Playboy, pornographic photographs, and a ballpoint pen with a picture of a naked woman that Dima had bought from tourists.

Project: NOVEMBER 11, 1974

Our second child is born in November. We name her after Bábushka Polina. She will be toilet-trained in a year which means we can shoot for early 1976 as our departure date.

ALEX: By 12 months, most Soviet children were completely toilet-trained—a big help in a society of cloth diapers and communal apartments.

BENA: Dima's mother is to come with us; my parents will follow after we get out. If we are denied permission, as refuseniks we will be outlaws. But my parents will still be legitimate citizens who could help us. My mother says:

ALEX: *(firmly)* "Do not feel guilty. Get the children out. The rest is irrelevant."
  (Pause)
The domestic winds blew in their favor. No sage or scholar or virulent anti-Semite at heart, Brezhnev was a godsend. Bushy-browed and draped in over a hundred decorations, he showed signs of having suffered a stroke.

BENA: We pray for his well-being. Spider sense tells us that his successor will not be as benign.

ALEX: Western radio intimated that in return for the "Most Favored Nation" trade status and for American wheat, an increase in Jewish emigration was coming and perhaps in addition to places other than Israel.

Although, to keep up the guise of family reunification, the invitations would still have to come only from Israel and emigration would still "officially" be permitted only to Israel.

BENA: Dima says he could not endure living in Israel without being able to serve in the army. Who, except the doctors, would believe that such a healthy-looking man has heart problems?

ALEX: They did not realize then that he was already too old for the Israeli army.

BENA: Dima convinces us to go to the United States.

Project: 1975

ALEX: Seven invitations arrive from Israel.

BENA: *(with growing excitement)* We begin the process. First step is to voluntarily resign from our jobs and get a negative character reference. We collect various documents and complete paperwork we'll need to present.

We warn friends not to call us; we'll call them from a public phone. We keep an eye on the political tides that have the power to smooth out, speed up, toughen, or terminate our plans.

We monitor the grapevine bulletins, make new contacts among the emigrant cohort, go to the station to see them off and devour letters from them.

Their letters are the pony express of directives on: what to do and in what order; what to take with us; what bribes work on customs officers and border patrol; what to say and what not to say; how to behave during customs at the Ukrainian border station; and what the train rides through Czechoslovakia on the way to Vienna were like.

Austrian Chancellor Bruno Kreisky who happened to be Jewish allowed Austria to be a layover stop for Jews leaving the USSR.

ALEX: Meanwhile, Soviet citizens got blindsided by sudden shortages of bread, milk and other food staples. The queues for food convulsed with hatred of Jews who were blamed for the shortages since they were obviously buying up food to take to Israel. Milk disappeared before 8 in the morning.

BENA: The sword of Damocles hits below the belt when the shortage targets yellow onions in stores—there isn't much one can cook without onions. The prices in the farmers markets jump astronomically.

ALEX: "People that reek of onions...live beyond their means."

BENA: Dima is disappointed by the scarcity of his favorite onion-on-bread meal. Once, when I see him eating it, I cry hysterically — And, from that day on, I start hiding onions from him.

ALEX: Dima's favorite joke in America:
"Just a warning, Bena: I'm cutting myself a piece of onion. Don't get upset!"

Finally --

BENA: Polina is toilet-trained! And Dima and my father have collected most of the paperwork to submit with our application.

ALEX: These documents were proof that they did not owe money anywhere or had books checked out from the library.

Avram and Rakhil submitted the very first piece of paper in the formal application process — their consent for Bena to emigrate. Parents had to consent in order for their children to emigrate, even if the child was grown and married, even retired.

Avram and Rakhil made a big production of it:
they underlined the word "consent" twice, and affixed large signatures. This was their chance to tell their government, loud and clear, what they thought of it and they were not going to miss the opportunity!

BENA: A more common response from most parents: "Over my dead body. Consent to emigrate not given!"

ALEX: At the end of December, it was down to the last charade: providing proof of family lineage in common with the "relative" in Israel who had sent the invitation. The applicants called it a "Legend." It's not like any of this was real.

BENA: I invent a great-great-grandfather who went to Palestine after his divorce. His great-great-grandson is eager to reunite with me. I detail my phony Israeli family's story, including dates of births and marriages in a notebook.

According to the grapevine, the attorney appointed to review and approve the legend free of charge expects 10 rubles per person emigrating. 15 if she had to write the legend herself!

I place the money into her desk drawer that she keeps ajar. Also, the typist expects a bottle of perfume or a box of chocolates.
(an anxious sigh)
Now we are ready.

Animation for Scene 9 plays with music.

SCENE 10

Project: JANUARY 5, 1976

ALEX: Dima, fortified by Valium, submitted their and his mother's applications to O.V.I.R. The privilege of renouncing Soviet citizenship cost 800 rubles per passport holder.

BENA: 1,600 rubles for our family plus 800 for my mother-in-law. My monthly salary was 100 rubles. We borrow 300 rubles from each of three friends and vow to pay off the loans with American clothes.

The rumor mill estimates that we should expect a summons from O.V.I.R. in about three months to learn if our application was approved. We will then have three weeks to wrap up what we already refer to as our former life. We did not think about what would happen if we became refuseniks.

ALEX: There were no official lists but somehow everyone knew what was allowed or forbidden to bring out of the country. For example, address books must not have any domestic addresses in it, leaving empty address books.

BENA: And X-rays are forbidden!!! How will we communicate with foreign physicians about the girls' medical issues?

ALEX: Their doctor snuck their X-rays out of the hospital for them. The postcard with the summons to O.V.I.R. arrived. They were to report in three days.

Project: MARCH 26, 1976

BENA: After two restless nights, Dima and I, holding trembling hands, join a group of two dozen in the waiting room. Encouraged by the relieved faces of the families ahead of us, we enter the room behind a polished door. A man with a buzz-cut recites:

ALEX: *(recites monotonously)* "The Union of the Soviet Socialist Republics has charitably agreed to approve your unification with kin in the state of Israel. Exit visas to be issued on March 26 effective through April 14, provided all the fees are paid and photographs furnished."

BENA: We thank him and, with heads down, we back out into the waiting room.

ALEX: They received their visas authorizing exit from the Soviet Union. But Mila had a fever attack a few days later.
　　　(a tense pause)
They were granted permission to extend the exit date from April 14 to April 22 so Mila could recover.

BENA: The reality of our departure is closing in painfully on our dearest friends most of whom, incredibly, have clung to the fantasy that we had been just talking the talk. My lifelong girlfriend makes the sign of the cross over me:

ALEX: *(making the sign of the cross over Bena)* "Of course, you should leave. If I were Jewish, I would leave this accursed country."
　　　(Pause)
Next step: now that they had their exit visas, Bena and Dima needed to secure entry visas into Israel. The only place authorized

to represent the Government of Israel in the Soviet Union was the Dutch Embassy in Moscow.

Project: April 9, 1976

BENA: Dima and I arrive by train in Moscow early in the morning. Inside the Dutch embassy, a woman behind a window takes our exit visas and tells us to return at 3 p.m. to pick up our Israeli entry visas. Once we get to Rome, we'll apply for entry visas to the United States.

We deliver 27 pages with names and addresses of other families seeking an invitation from their Israeli "relatives". The Dutch Embassy will undiplomatically pass on those requests to the Israelis.

With a little time to kill before the 3 p.m. pick-up, we sprint over to the famously well-supplied Moscow department stores. In one, mounted militia control the mob of delirious women screaming out German bra sizes. We return to the Embassy, get our entry visas and board the train for the ride back to Kiev.

Project: April 13, 1976

ALEX: Packing time for items to be shipped!

BENA: *(all business)*
Books.
Bookcase wall unit.
Pillows.
Kitchen stuff.
Blankets.
Photos.

Several cuts of fabric.
Two wall rugs.

And I know how helpful odds and ends can be: threads, shirt buttons, shoelaces, and zippers to replace broken ones. In America, every unspent penny will help.

It takes a KGB captain many hours to examine our 3,500 books, one by one. He shakes each book, squeezes its back, checks the year of publication, and ascertains that it does not belong to a library.

The inspection of our photographs goes faster: we have none showing bridges or people in military uniforms.

ALEX: The Hebrew Immigrant Aid Society - HIAS - picked up the cost of shipping up to a metric ton of household goods – a thousand kilos.

BENA: Our stuff weighs in at 920 kilos. The official fee for the delivery of our luggage to the dock and for packing the crates comes to 30 rubles. The movers ask for 300 rubles under the table and, of course, a meal to take care of our -- in their words -- pathetic belongings.

ALEX: Bena never forgave the three wardrobe-shaped men for devouring all their food which was intended to last them for a week.

Project: APRIL 14, 1976

As allowed by the government, they exchanged 100 rubles per person into $90. They had never seen foreign currency before!

Rumor recommended that men stay inside so as not to fall victim to provoked fights which would trigger a fifteen-day detention and rescindment of permission to leave. Dima did not leave the house that last week.

BENA: We surrender our apartment effective April 20. Our visas entitle us to purchase one-way train tickets for the route Kiev – Chop – Bratislava – Vienna.

Project: APRIL 16, 1976

ALEX: The final task! They needed to hand over all their documents to the Kiev City Archive since originals were not allowed out of the country. With each passing day, it appeared less likely that things could fall apart for them. But, it was still possible.

BENA: *(tense sigh)* At the City Archives, the clerk discovers a discrepancy in the spelling of my first name. On my copy of my birth certificate, it is spelled B-e-n-a and on the original birth certificate on file there it is spelled B-e-n-n-a.

ALEX: *(woodenly)* "You are not you. A notary must confirm that you are you."

BENA: She gives me the address of a notary office that handles amendments to emigrants' documents. I arrive there and say I need authentication that I am well, me

ALEX: "Come after lunch with chocolates for the typist. I'll issue a *spravka* that you are you."

Once proven that B-e-n-a and B-e-n-n-a were one and the same person, the archive accepted the documents and issued a receipt. Bena delivered the stack of paperwork to O.V.I.R.

BENA: *(excited)* We are Soviet citizens no more!

    (jittery)
We are now stateless.

    Animation for Scene 10 plays with music.

SCENE 11

ALEX: A long line forms in a store waiting for salami. Finally, the manager comes out:

"Comrades, we won't get as much salami as we hoped. So, it will not be available to Jews." The Jews leave.

In an hour, the manager announces: "Salami will only be available to war veterans." The crowd thins.

In another hour: "Salami will only be for war veterans who are members of the Communist Party." A small group remains.

Sometime later: "Sorry, comrades, we'll get no salami today, after all."

Everyone remaining in the line screams: "Again, Jews had all the luck! They didn't have to wait so long."

Project: APRIL 20, 1976 – the final day in Kiev

BENA: As we get into the two cabs to go to the train station, a few curtains stir from our apartment building. My parents and a small gathering see the five of us off at the railroad station.

Project: APRIL 21, 1976 – Chop, Ukraine border station with Slovakia, then-part of Czechoslovakia.

The border station is empty, the door to customs is locked until 10 in the evening, an hour before the train to Bratislava is scheduled to depart. Previous emigrants have equipped us with advice as precise as a recipe.

Dima finds the recommended luggage handler. For 30 rubles he will load our suitcases onto a cart the moment customs release them; jog to the car number shown on the ticket; and persuade the engineer to dilly-dally if my mother-in-law is not able to walk fast enough to board.

Customs opens. Three officers wait behind a metal table stretching the length of the room. Dima places the suitcases on the table. An older officer strolls over:

ALEX: *(spitefully)* "Today is April 21! And you're not embarrassed?"

BENA: We stare in panic.

ALEX: "Tomorrow is Lenin's birthday! Couldn't you wait to leave for a couple days?"

BENA: We lower our heads – it is prudent to display guilt. In slow motion, he examines our documents. And with a practiced move, he takes two bottles of vodka from us
　　　(with a wry smile)
which are purposely above the limit of two bottles per person. He slides them under the table.

Now Dima is pushing the suitcase containing Mila's and Polina's forbidden X-rays toward another officer who assumes a gotcha expression when he sees them. But Dima's body language displays trust and intimacy. Referring to our doctor's statement, he recaps the girls' medical issues.

ALEX: *(as the Officer, narrowing his eyes suspiciously)* "How do I know this is not a picture of something military?"

(now as Dima)
"But you would know. You are an intelligent man."

BENA: *(relieved)* Stupefied by Dima's compliment, the officer throws the X-rays back into the suitcase as if letting through a batch of Kalashnikovs. We are cleared.

ALEX: Turns out the doctors in Vienna and Rome could not read the X-rays because the quality was so poor.

BENA: Our luggage handler goes beyond what 30 rubles bought; he hands the suitcases to Dima through the train window. The train does not have to dilly-dally.

Project: APRIL 22, 1976 – Bratislava

BENA: Getting off the train in Bratislava, we decide to dip into our American currency to feed the girls at the train station's café. The waitress feeds us like royalty for only one dollar.

The staff surrounds the table and quizzes us, in Russian, about the trick we utilized to get away from Big Brother. As we get up to leave they applaud. A waiter is galloping to the platform to bring us the stuffed poodle that Polina left behind along with some pastries for the road.

ALEX: At the Austrian border two Austrian policemen board the train for protection. Arab groups protesting immigration to Israel had in the past attempted terrorist acts against Soviet Jews arriving in Austria.

BENA: The presence of the older officer – a big barrel-chested man – brings home the fact that we have made it out, once and for all.

(palms together bowing to him; almost hysterically)
"Danke! Danke! Danke!"
(Pause)

ALEX: It was not giddiness. It was deliverance.

BENA: Moved to tears, the policeman sits with us, rifle between his knees. He shows off pictures of his children and grandchildren and predicts a magnificent future awaiting us. Then he returns to his post at the door, beaming at us all the way to Vienna.

Now we can tell Mila that she is Jewish and has every reason to be proud of it. Seven years old, her observations have already taught her otherwise. Only a few weeks earlier, she approved of her classmates beating up a boy "for being Jewish" – we have carried her off in the nick of time.

ALEX: As the train approached Vienna, Bena indulged in daydreaming about fresh vegetables at the height of off-season, at least carrots and cabbage. All the letters said that there were no shortages here.

Project: APRIL 22, 1976 – Vienna, Austria

BENA: When we get off the train, four men from HIAS ask us in Russian what country we have chosen. Dima says America.

ALEX: Immigrants spent three weeks in Vienna which involved reams of paperwork at HIAS.

BENA: The men load our luggage into a van with a driver who looks like a heavy-weight boxer.

We are driven to an old five-story building, a former bordello. A lively woman hands Dima a key to a room with a bathroom on the fourth floor. I ask Dima to see if any store might possibly have milk left at 1 in the afternoon. He returns, empty-handed but exuberant:

ALEX: *(breathlessly)* "Let's go! You won't believe it!"

BENA: We clamber down the stairs and cross the street. Dima drags me into a store. Not a store – a palace: bright lights, colorful packages, pretty-labeled jars of every configuration, fresh produce in clean bins where customers are allowed to pick, and an entire wall dedicated to dairy.

ALEX: Yes, they had milk at 1 in the afternoon.

BENA: Not one empty shelf. A few unhurried customers. And carts on wheels to place purchases in. Not sure if we need permission, we take one. We are gasping as we see pictures of fruit on yogurt containers. Yogurt could have fruit in it!

The next day begins with a trip to the farmer's market. I am feeling dizzy as my eyes fall on crates displaying rows of chicken livers, wings, breasts— a crate for each chicken part.
The lines are short and the people in them are calm. I pay the seller.

ALEX: *(politely)* "*Danke schon.*"

BENA: Am I hallucinating? He gives me chicken livers and <u>he</u> is thanking <u>me</u>?

ALEX: *(politely, impatiently)* "*Danke schon*".

BENA: I just stand there frozen. Dima has to pull me away. We are surrounded by a reality where everything is happening for the first time. From the Post Office, I call my parents in Kiev to tell them about the salesman thanking us and the chicken parts sold separately. My mother does not believe me.

Animation for Scene 11 plays with music.

SCENE 12

Project: MAY 6, 1976 – Rome, Italy

ALEX: The final layover.

BENA: Two buses chartered by HIAS are bringing us, a hundred Soviet immigrants, from Vienna to Rome.

ALEX: They spent over four months there learning English, meeting with their caseworker, sightseeing, and waiting for their entry visas into the United States.

BENA: Dima finds a room in a three-room apartment in Ostia Lido, a beachfront suburb, half-hour train ride from Rome. HIAS will pay for it until we leave for the United States.

Our caseworker, Mrs. Miller, is the first American I have ever met. She speaks Russian! In her fifties, tall, slim, tanned, with boyish hair that is meticulously styled. In spite of her old age by Soviet standards, she has the guts to wear pants, fitted tops, and necklaces made from large painted wooden beads. She does not act elderly, either.

Are all old American women like her? Will I be like her in 25 years? In turn, Mrs. Miller is impressed that we try to speak and fill out paperwork in English.

ALEX: Mrs. Miller gave Dima and Mila American names: Mike and Emily. She said that Bena sounded fine but Polina should be Pauline or Paula.

BENA: "I won't spell or pronounce Bábushka's name differently!"

ALEX: Before she chucked their file into a proverbial hat to be plucked by a random American Jewish community that would take them in, they had to complete a form indicating their choices for where they preferred to live.

BENA: We have no right to be choosy, but it will be easier to find a job in a larger city. Except New York, if possible. We have heard that one does not need to know English to live there and we do not want that.

Project: JULY 1976 – Rome, Italy

ALEX: The United States turns 200. Bena turns 31.

BENA: *(upset)* Mrs. Miller tells us that the Chicago Jewish community will sponsor us. We are crushed. Chicago means gangs and slaughterhouses! But Mrs. Miller thinks that our information is outdated.

ALEX: "I'm from Chicago myself and I personally recommended you. It's a great city. If you don't find a job in Chicago, you won't find it anywhere. Jewish Family and Community Services – JFCS - - will take good care of you."
     (Pause)
HIAS supplied a brochure, in English and Russian: "Entering a New Culture: A Handbook for Soviet Migrants to the United States of America". The brochure was priceless:

BENA: Many things go over our heads especially learning that in America Jewish is a religion and not a nationality.

ALEX: They also learned that:

BENA: Americans react negatively to body or mouth odors;
Tip 15 percent in restaurants;
Write the number 7 without the bar across the middle;
Do not ask money-related questions;
Consider a smile very important; and
Being left-handed is permitted.

ALEX: *(with pride)* A year later, HIAS and the Jewish Federation in Chicago asked Bena to update the brochure.

Project: SEPTEMBER 14, 1976 – Rome, Italy

BENA: A HIAS person delivers us to the airport in Rome, checks in our luggage, and walks us to the gate of our Alitalia flight to New York. We spend the night in a motel near Kennedy airport.

Project: SEPTEMBER 15, 1976 – Chicago, USA

At 5 a.m., another HIAS person shepherds us onto a bus, through luggage drop-off and to the gate of our <u>American</u> Airlines flight to Chicago. Two hours later we see Chicago from above. So much greenery, not just gangs and slaughterhouses!

At the gate, a man from HIAS greets us and drives us to East Rogers Park. He points to a four-story building and gives us a key to a one-bedroom furnished apartment where JFCS has delivered two brand-new mattresses as a gift. We sign for a $10 bill he produces. On a scrap of paper, he scribbles:

ALEX: "Tomorrow, 9 a.m., J.F.C.S., 2710 West Devon Avenue."

BENA: We find a supermarket called Jewel *(stress on Jew)* a block away. The door opens automatically as we approach—what a welcome! Vienna and Rome have educated us on shopping carts, plastic bags and politeness, but we are not prepared for the American supermarket phenomenon. Enthralled, we weave through the store, holding hands, afraid to get lost. How does one know how to find anything? Food specifically for pets?

ALEX: Emily cried. She remembered waiting for two hours in a line for chicken in Kiev and getting nothing.

BENA: The next morning, we stand on the corner, showing the address for JFCS to passersby to no avail. Finally, an older man motions to follow him. He speaks to us slowly in a mix of Yiddish and English.

ALEX: "*Kum mit mir. Ich bin ein* dentist. *Ich arbeit* in the same building."

BENA: He pays our bus fare and we thank him — in Yiddish.

ALEX: "When did you come?"

BENA: Dima tells him our story trying not to use Russian words. People in the street are wearing odd clothes. I've never seen clothes like that before, even in pictures.

ALEX: *(noticing Bena's surprised demeanor)* "A lot of Orthodox Jews live here in West Rogers Park.
     (pause)
Zoll sein mit mazel."
     (Alex exits)

BENA: An eerie sense of déjà vu floods over me. I notice a man with a long beard, dressed in black wearing a hat that I recognize

from Bábushka's description as the kind of hat her father Velvel --
my great-grandfather — wore — a *shtreimel*.
    (matter-of-factly and with a slight smile)
I am home.

Animation for Scene 12 plays with music.

SCENE 13

BENA: *(present time)* On May 5, 1977, my parents, Avram and Rakhil, landed in Chicago. When they got off the plane, a camera-clicking and microphone-thrusting group surrounded them. My parents were the thousandth Soviet immigrants to Chicago!

We Soviet Jews were an enigma to American Jews. They thought we had risked everything for the freedom to maintain Jewish traditions. But when we gained that freedom, it turned out we didn't really know that we had traditions.
　　(she chuckles a little)
Once, I sent Emily and Polina off to their Orthodox Jewish day school with their lunch packed: Pork chops. I couldn't understand why the principal was outraged. I even asked:

"How do you spell Kosher?"

American Jews saw an unknown species in us - their cousins from behind the Iron Curtain. Many decades of life on different planets can do that to a family. But only for a time. Then we're one family again.
　　(pause)
How many bushels are my children worth?
How many bushels are my five grandchildren worth?
　　(pause)
How many bushels am I worth?

END OF PLAY